Spelling Rules!

Janelle Ho and
Helen Pearson

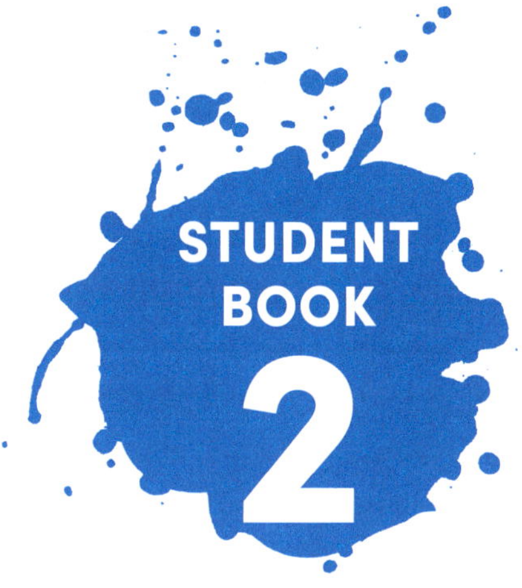

NSW Edition

Name: ______________________________

Class: ______________________________

Contents

SLLURP

SLLURP summarises the spelling strategies that you can use to learn new words.

Say	Say the word carefully and slowly to yourself.
Listen	Listen to how each part of the word sounds in sequence.
Look	Look at the patterns of letters in the word and the shape of the word.
Understand	Understand rules, word meanings and word origins.
Remember	Remember all the similar words you can already spell and relate this knowledge to any new word.
Practise	Practise writing the word until it is firmly fixed in your long-term memory.

Scope and Sequence

This scope and sequence chart is based on the requirements of the NSW Curriculum.

Unit	Skill Focus: Vowels	Consonants	Letter patterns	Morphology	Homophones/ Homographs	Topic words	Word List
1	split digraphs: a-e, i-e, o-e, e-e, u-e	blends and digraphs		-ed, -ing: dropping final 'e'			place, scrape, time, unite, slope, whole, complete, squeeze, rule, cure
2	short vowel sounds	blends and digraphs		-ed, -ing: doubling final consonant			beg, scan, clap, strap, swim, begin, block, throb, thud, scrub
3	semi-vowel y			-es, -ed: changing 'y' to 'i'			lady, pony, busy, ready, sorry, worry, carry, hurry, reply, apply
4			ar	-er, -est			arm, car, park, dark, star, start, hard, barn, smart, farmer
5		medial double letters					letter, little, bottle, rabbit, cuddle, riddle, ripple, tunnel, borrow, pillow
6		ck, medial ck					chicken, bucket, ticket, packet, pocket, jacket, cricket, bracket, backpack, limerick
7	REVISION						
8		tch, medial tch		-es			itchy, witch, stitch, catch, hatch, watch, fetch, stretch, hutch, kitchen
9		dge, medial dge					edge, hedge, badge, fridge, bridge, judge, smudge, dodge, fidget, gadget
10			or, ore	compound words: fore-	for/four/fore		for, fork, torn, short, sport, more, fore, snore, chore, explore
11			aw, oor				saw, draw, claw, straw, crawl, lawn, prawn, poor, door, floor
12			ar, al	-ward/-wards			war, warn, ward, swarm, award, reward, towards, walk, talk, chalk
13			ough, augh	irregular verbs			ought, bought, brought, fought, thought, sought, caught, taught, naughty, daughter
14	REVISION						
15			silent letters: kn, wr, silent 't'				knife, knowledge, wrong, wrist, wriggle, listen, often, castle, bustle, whistle
16			air, are, ear	compound words: air-	stare/stair, bare/ bear, where/wear		pair, stair, chair, repair, airport, rare, share, square, wear, bear
17			ear, eer		tear, wind, bow; hear/here, dear/deer		fear, hear, tear, clear, spear, weary, appear, deer, peer, cheer, queer
18			er, ir	-er, -est: practising spelling rules			fern, serve, person, perfect, stir, shirt, first, dirty, thirsty, birthday
19			ear, or, ur				turn, hurt, burst, nurse, curly, work, worth, learn, earth, search
20				-er, -or: practising spelling rules		people, occupations	farmer, leader, shopper, follower, visitor, collector, editor, author, narrator, illustrator
21	REVISION						
22				re-, un-, dis-			redo, reread, rejoin, reunite, unkind, unfair, untidy, disagree, disappear, disobey
23	u, o						lung, pluck, under, love, done, above, front, month, among, money
24	ou, oo			-er, -est			young, touch, cousin, country, double, rough, tough, enough, flood, blood
25				-ful: changing 'y' to 'i'			joyful, useful, playful, cheerful, helpful, careful, painful, awful, colourful, beautiful
26				-ly: changing 'y' to 'i'			sadly, loudly, slowly, nicely, rudely, quickly, quietly, crossly, kindly, happily
27						days of the week	Monday, Tuesday, Wednesday, Thursday, Friday, Saturday, Sunday, today, tomorrow, because
28	REVISION						
29	o, a, au						foggy, along, belong, toffee, homophone, wasp, wand, watch, wander, sausage
30				contractions			I'll, he's, it's, isn't, can't, don't, doesn't, didn't, won't, we're
31		soft c			cents/scent, scene/seen		city, cent, scent, scene, once, cancel, cycle, cylinder, science, scissors
32		silent letters: mb, mn					lamb, limb, dumb, numb, thumb, comb, climb, autumn, column, plumber
33		ch				compound words with ache	school, ache, choir, character, chorus, chameleon, stomach, anchor, chef, machine
34						compound words with no, any, some, every	no one, nothing, nowhere, somebody, something, anyone, anything, another, everyone, everywhere
35	REVISION						

NOTE TO TEACHERS AND PARENTS

Spelling Rules!

Some students are natural spellers. But the vast majority of students need formal, systematic and sequential instruction about the way spelling works and the strategies they can use to become independent, confident spellers.

The *Spelling Rules!* program is based on sound linguistic and pedagogical theory. It is informed by research into how students of different ages acquire and apply spelling skills, and how those skills move from the working to the long-term memory. The program closely follows the NSW English Curriculum. NSW Curriculum references are provided in the two Teacher Resource Books. The program consists of seven Student Books.

Each student book contains units of work, with each unit designed to be used over the course of a week. The content of each unit follows the suggested instructional sequence in the NSW English syllabus. Each unit simultaneously develops new skills and reinforces skills from previous units. Where appropriate, topic words from other curriculum areas are included. When spelling rules and tips are introduced, only known sounds and letter patterns are used so that students focus on one skill at a time. Regular revision units enable teachers to assess student progress and reinforce key rules and patterns from previous units. Books 1 to 6 also include a simple reflection activity that encourages students to assess their own progress and provides you with a starting point for discussion.

Spelling knowledge

Learning to spell involves developing different kinds of spelling knowledge:

- **Kinaesthetic knowledge** – the physical feeling when saying different sounds and words, and when writing the shapes of letters and words
- **Phonological knowledge** – how a word sounds and the patterns of sounds in words
- **Visual knowledge** – how letters and words look and the visual patterns in words
- **Morphemic knowledge** – the meaning or function of words or parts of words
- **Etymological knowledge** – the origins and history of words and the effect this has on spelling patterns.

Icons used in Student Book 2

The following icons identify the main spelling strategy that students will use to complete an activity.

Say the word. (Kinaesthetic knowledge) These activities ask students to experience how sounds feel in the mouth and jaw. Changing the positions of the jaw, lips and tongue changes the sounds we make. Encourage students to pronounce the sounds and words accurately. If they mispronounce a sound or word, they may misrepresent it in writing.

Listen to the word. (Phonological knowledge) These activities focus on discriminating between different sounds and breaking up words into syllables or individual sound segments (phonemes).

Look at the word. (Visual knowledge) These activities help students to see how the sound is represented using combinations of letters, and to associate this visual pattern with what they are hearing. Students will develop the ability to know when a word does or does not 'look right'.

Understand the word. (Morphemic and etymological knowledge) These activities focus on word meanings, word families, prefixes and suffixes, spelling rules, word origins and so on, which help embed spelling in the long-term memory.

Practise writing the word. (Kinaesthetic knowledge) These activities develop students' awareness of the physical movement involved in writing the word. By practising writing the word a number of times and in different contexts, the spelling becomes embedded in the long-term memory.

This icon highlights useful spelling rules.

This icon tells students that a special clue or hint is provided for an activity. It may be a spelling, grammar or punctuation convention, or a definition of a useful term.

Encourages students to assess their progress across each unit.

Student Book 2

Units of work

Student Book 2 contains 35 weekly units of work. Groups of units focus on different phonemes that represent the same sound. The suffixes taught in Book 1 are consolidated using new words. They are also elaborated on by using spelling rules such as the dropping of silent 'e' and the doubling of the final consonant. More suffixes (*ful, ly*) and prefixes (*re, un, dis*) are taught and homophones are explained and practised. Finally, the concepts of irregular verbs, silent letters and contractions are also presented. See the **Scope and Sequence chart** on page 3 for more information.

Word lists

In *Student Book 2*, each unit (except Revision) has a list of ten spelling words. The words are selected to support the learning focus and spelling strategies in the unit. The list also includes words from other curriculum areas such as mathematics, science and social sciences. Where appropriate, Aboriginal Australian English words are also included.

SLLURP

Each word list begins with a reminder for students to SLLURP. SLLURP summarises the strategies that will help spelling move from students' working memory to their long-term memory. These strategies are provided on page 2, for easy reference.

Unit at a glance

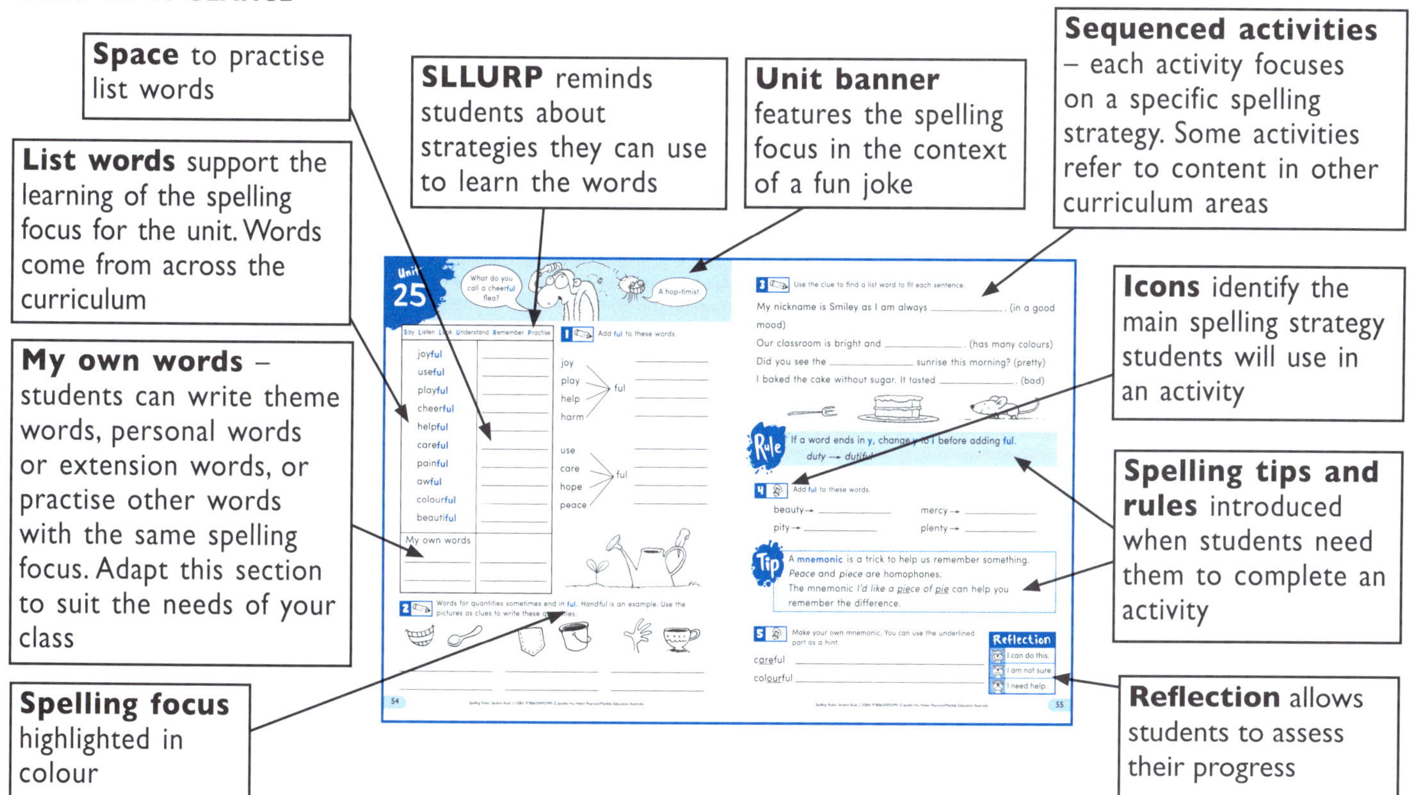

Spelling Rules! Teacher Resource Book K–2

Full teacher support for *Student Book 2* is provided by *Spelling Rules! Teacher Resource Book K–2*. Here you will find valuable background information about spelling development and spelling knowledge, along with practical resources, such as:

- teaching tips for every unit in *Student Book 2*
- extra word lists
- strategies for teaching spelling
- guidelines for assessing and diagnosing errors
- activities to support struggling spellers
- worthwhile extension for more able spellers.

Unit 1

What snake is good at sums?

An adder.

Say Listen Look Understand Remember Practise	
place	
scrape	
time	
unite	
slope	
whole	
complete	
squeeze	
rule	
cure	
My own words	

1 Write list words in the correct tree.

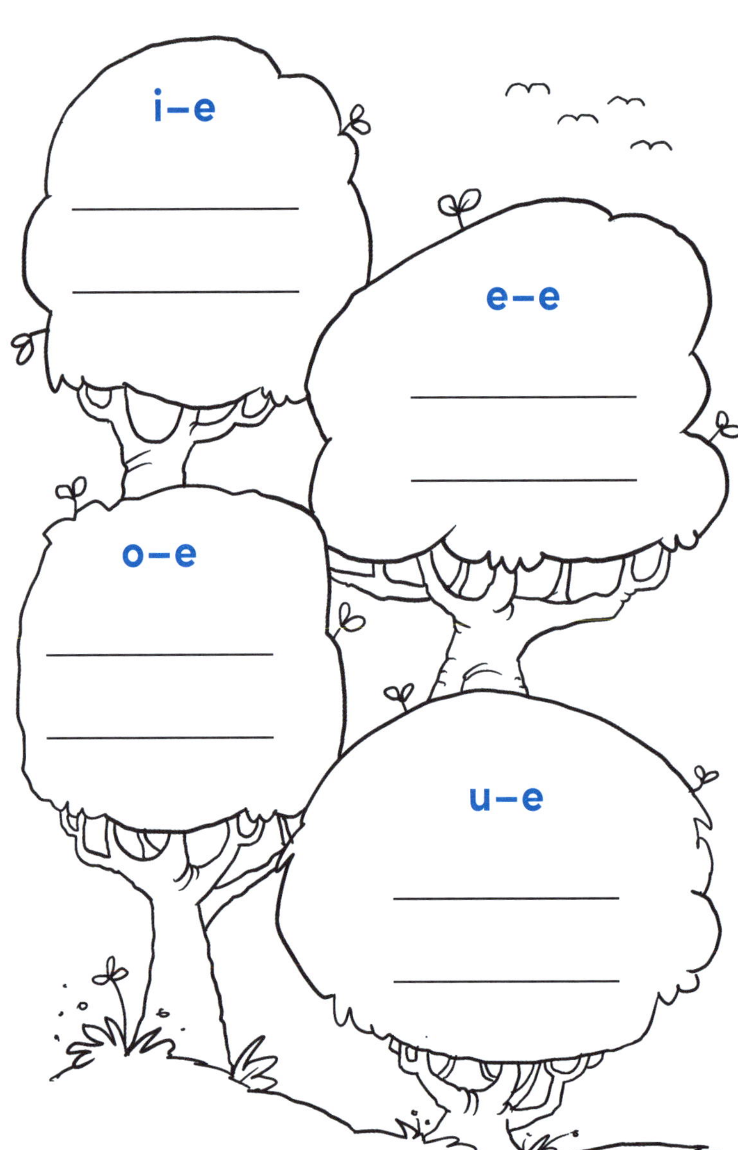

2 Write the word. Then write it again, adding **e** to change the vowel sound.

welcome

Spelling Rules! Student Book 2 (ISBN 9780655092599) © Janelle Ho, Helen Pearson/Matilda Education Australia

 Write two words that begin with the same sound as the picture.

	list word	extra word		list word	extra word
	______	______		______	______
	______	______		______	______

Homophones are words that sound the same, but are spelt differently.

hole = empty space

whole = all of

 Choose the correct homophone.

Shane ate the ______ cake.

Jane dug a ______ in the sand.

I tore a ______ in my pants.

Did you see the ______ movie?

 Look for small words inside the list word. Write the small words.

place ______ ______

whole ______ ______

unite ______ ______ ______

Words with a silent **e** drop the **e** before adding **ed** or **ing**.

Smiling, the monkey waved at me.

 Follow the pattern.

plac~~e~~ + **ed** = **placed** place + **ing** = **placing**

unit~~e~~ + **ed** = ______ unit~~e~~ + **ing** = ______

rul~~e~~ + **ed** = ______ rul~~e~~ + **ing** = ______

squeez~~e~~ + **ed** = ______

squeez~~e~~ + **ing** = ______

Reflection

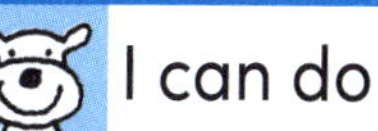 I can do this.

 I am not sure.

 I need help.

Unit 2

Why couldn't the leopard escape from the zoo?

Because he was always spott**ed**.

Say **L**isten **L**ook **U**nderstand **R**emember **P**ractise	
beg	________
scan	________
clap	________
strap	________
swim	________
begin	________
block	________
throb	________
thud	________
scrub	________
My own words	
________	________
________	________

1 Write the vowels in the first column. Then write words with short and long vowels to fill in the spaces.

vowels	short sound	long sound
a	mad	________
____	________	Pete
____	________	slide
____	hop	________
____	________	huge

Rule

If a word has a short vowel sound and ends in a single consonant, double the consonant before adding **ed** or **ing**.

2 Write the word when **ing** is added.

beg ________ strap ________ throb ________

scan ________ begin ________ thud ________

clap ________ scrub ________ block ________

 Circle the pictures that have short vowel sounds.

 Write the missing letter.

beg ___ ed	rub ___ ed	spot ___ ed	plan ___ ed
pat ___ ed	stop ___ ed	skip ___ ed	hum ___ ed

Most words add **ed** to make the past tense. Some words change. They are called **irregular verbs**. *swim* → *swam*

 Follow the pattern.

swim	sing	stink	begin	drink
swam	s ___ ng	st ______	beg ______	______

6 Write a sentence for each word.

thudded ______________________________

____

____

began ______________________________

____

____

Reflection

 I can do this.

 I am not sure.

 I need help.

Unit 3

What beans can't you grow in a garden?

Say Listen Look Understand Remember Practise

lady	________
pony	________
busy	________
ready	________
sorry	________
worry	________
carry	________
hurry	________
reply	________
apply	________
My own words	
________	________
________	________

1 Draw a line between each sound. Underline each syllable.

lady busy ready

sorry worry hurry

carry reply apply

2 Say each list word. Sort the words by the sound y makes.

y in puppy

________ ________

________ ________

________ ________

________ ________

y in cry

________ ________

3 Write a list word for each group. Add another word ending in a short y sound.

animals	people	feelings	actions
bunny	aunty	angry	study
________	________	________	________
________	________	________	________

Spelling Rules! Student Book 2 (ISBN 9780655092599) © Janelle Ho, Helen Pearson/Matilda Education Australia

Proofread this story. The story has six words that are incorrect. Circle the mistakes. Then write the correct spelling of the words in the boxes.

Tony's front tooth was wobly. When it fell out, he lost it. He was not heppy as he planned to put it under his pillow for the tooth fairy. Tony felt silly, but he decided to write a not.

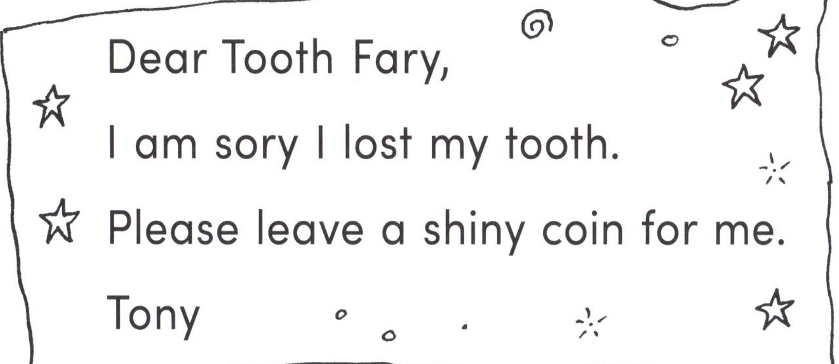

In the morning Tony rubed his eyes and felt under his pillow. He found two dollars! Wasn't he lucky?

If a word ends in **y**, change **y** to **i** before adding **es** or **ed**.
To make the plural, add **es**. *lady → ladies*
To change the verb, add **es** or **ed**.
worry → worries, worried *cry → cries, cried*

Write the word when **es** or **ed** is added.

plural		past tense	
pony	____________	carry	____________
baby	____________	reply	____________
		apply	____________

Unit 4

Say Listen Look Understand Remember Practise	
arm	______
car	______
park	______
dark	______
star	______
start	______
hard	______
barn	______
smart	______
farmer	______
My own words	
______	______
______	______

1 Make ar words.

ark: sh, b, m, d, p

______
______
______
______
______

art: st, ch, m, d, p

______
______
______
______
______

2 Find a small word in the big word. Write a different small word for each.

card ______ start ______ bark ______

harm ______ barn ______ cart ______

farmer ______ heart ______ father ______

3 Finish the letter.

hard	far	farm	dark	barn	yard

Dear Uncle Carl,

I loved staying on your ________. It was so ________ at night! I liked hunting for eggs in the ________ and in the ________. It was ________ to find them in the long grass. I wish you did not live so ________ away.

Love from Mark

X X X

Tip Adjectives are describing words. To compare two things, add **er** to an adjective. To compare three or more things, add **est**.

fast *faster* *fastest*

4 There are three adjectives in the list words. Write them down. Add **er** and **est**.

list word	________	________	________
add **er**	________	________	________
add **est**	________	________	________

5 Circle two mistakes.

The farmer caried his shepe to the barn.

Unit 5

What do you call a nervous insect?

A jitterbug.

Say Listen Look Understand Remember Practise	
letter	____________
little	____________
bottle	____________
rabbit	____________
cuddle	____________
riddle	____________
ripple	____________
tunnel	____________
borrow	____________
pillow	____________
My own words	
____________	____________
____________	____________

1 The words in each ladder are missing the same double letters. Write the missing letters.

ss
tt
nn
ll

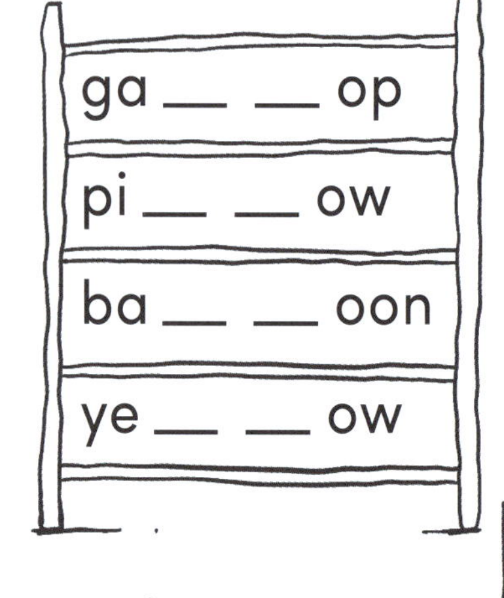

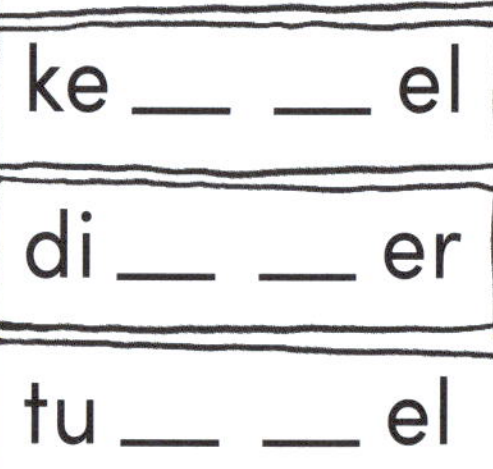

le __ __ er
bu __ __ er
ki __ __ en

2 Change one letter to make a new word.

~~l~~etter + b = ____________

b~~o~~ttle + a = ____________

b~~o~~rrow + u = ____________

m~~u~~ddle + i = ____________

~~g~~iggle + wr = ____________

~~j~~uggle + str = ____________

Write a list word.

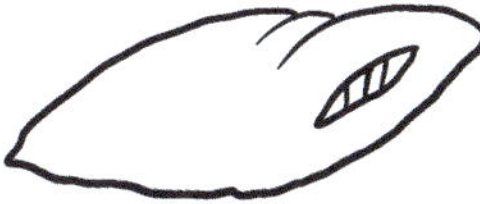

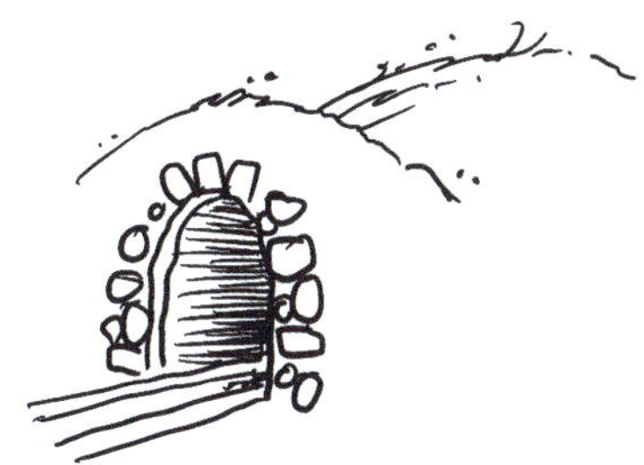

__________ __________ __________ __________

4 Write new double letters to make another word.

puzzle dribble riddle

pu __ __ le dri __ __ le __________

5 Write a vowel to make different words.

f __ llow l __ tter b __ rrow

f __ llow l __ tter b __ rrow

b __ rrow

Write double consonants to find what William's family is cooking for Grandpa's birthday.

It is Grandpa's birthday tomorrow. We went shopping and bought his favourite foods.

There will be a salad with le __ __ uce and ca __ __ ot. Dad will make Grandma's special po __ __ um nu __ __ ets spiced with wa __ __ le seeds. For de __ __ ert, Aunty will bake her a __ __ le and bluebe __ __ y pie. The adults will likely have co __ __ ee after di __ __ er. We think Grandpa will eat it all!

Reflection

 I can do this.

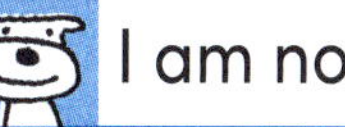 I am not sure.

I need help.

Unit 6

Say Listen Look Understand Remember Practise	
chicken	____________
bucket	____________
ticket	____________
packet	____________
pocket	____________
jacket	____________
cricket	____________
bracket	____________
backpack	____________
limerick	____________
My own words	
____________	____________
____________	____________

1 Find a list word for each shape.

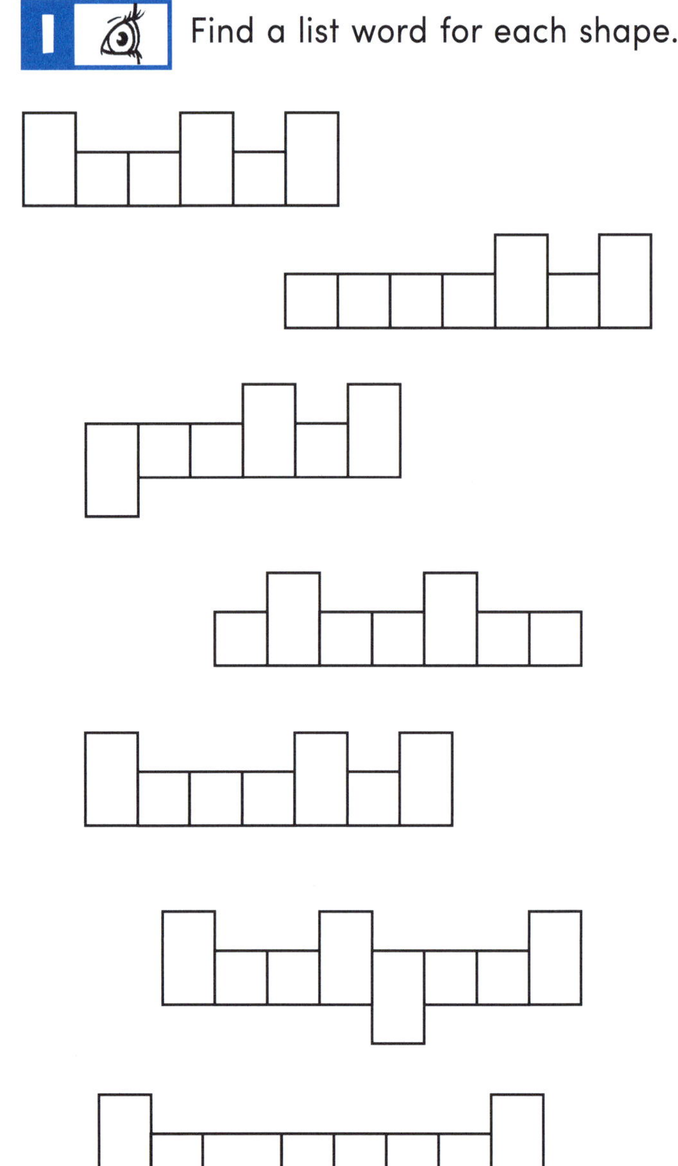

2 Write list words that rhyme.

rocket	wicket	packet
____________	____________	____________
	____________	____________

3 Use the first vowel to put list words in the correct bucket.

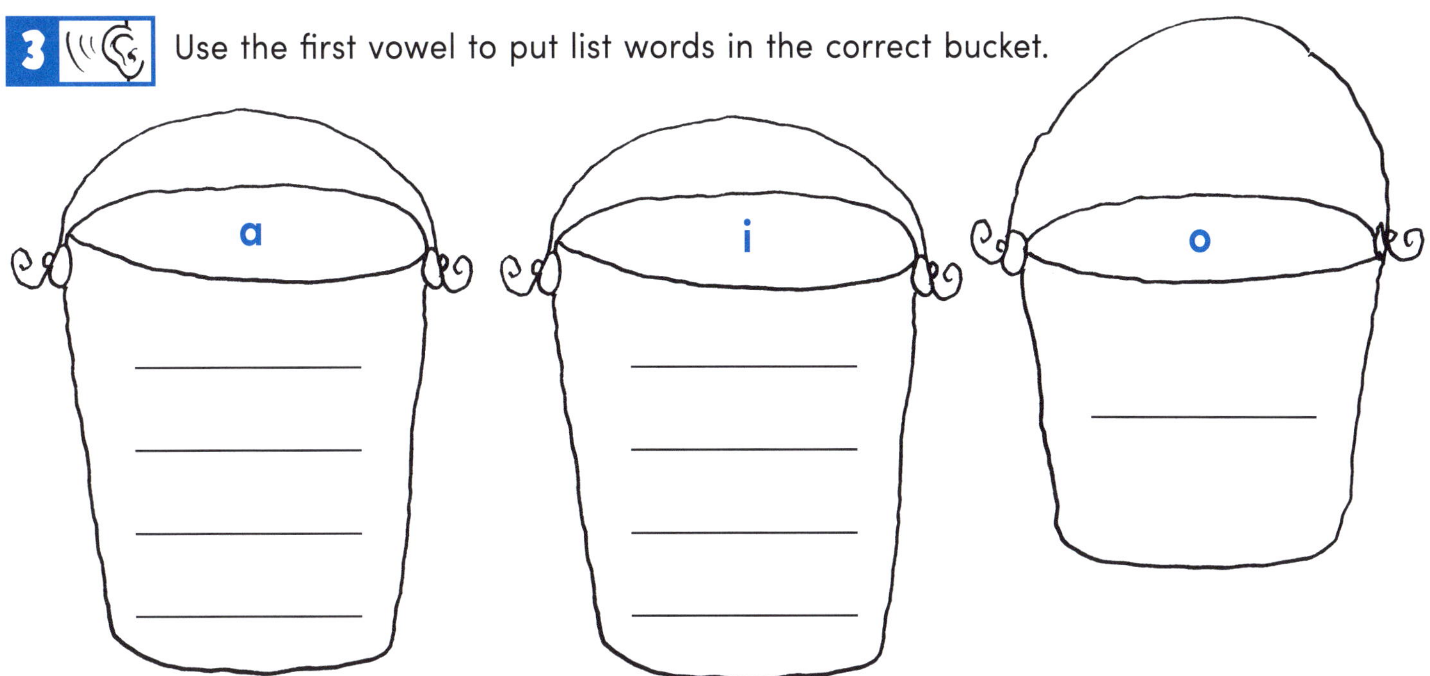

Words that end in **ck** add **ed** to make the past tense.
The number of syllables do not change.

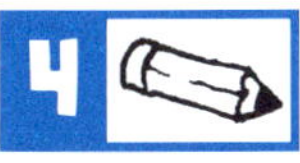

4 Change one letter at a time to make a new word. The first set is done for you.

jacket	packed	locked	packet
packet	________	________	________
pocket	________	________	________
docket	socket	ticket	kicked

5 Say the word. Write the number of syllables in the circle.

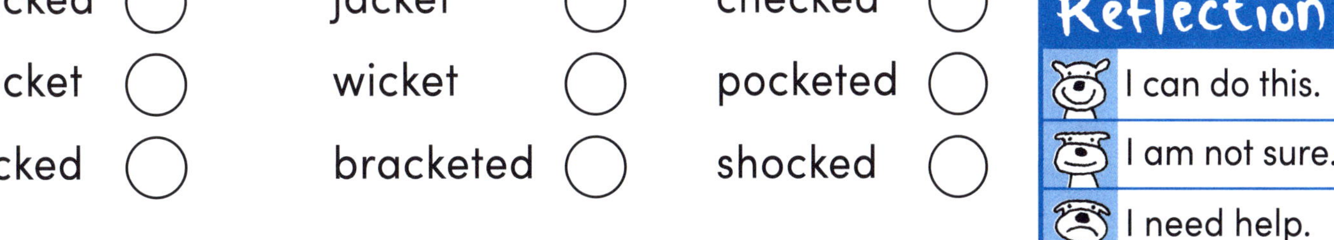

 Say each word. Circle the word in each column that has a different vowel sound.

borrow	lady	beg	time	cuddle
pocket	carry	squeeze	little	bucket
worry	jacket	letter	ticket	busy

 Write the word. Remember your spelling rules!

add **ed**		add **ing**	
apply	____________	hurry	____________
blame	____________	chase	____________
cuddle	____________	ripple	____________
scrub	____________	thud	____________
worry	____________	reply	____________

 Use the clue to make a list word.

Add one letter to *scrap*. ____________

Add two letters to *beg*. ____________

Change one letter in *pocket*. ____________

Add two letters to *tick*. ____________

Remove one letter from *start*. ____________

Change one letter in *sorry*. ____________

Adjectives add **er** to compare two things. The **er** word is a comparative adjective. *loud louder* *soft softer*

Some words add **er** to make a person or a thing. The **er** word is a noun. *lead leader* *print printer*

Colour the words that are comparative adjectives in blue. Colour the words that are nouns in yellow.

cricketer	harder	worrier	swimmer	littler
beginner	busier	darker	readier	scanner

5 Use the meaning to write a list word.

begin ______________ end ______________

not soft ______________ not big ______________

the side of a hill ______________

word you use to say it is your fault ______________

This story has eight words that are incorrect. Circle the mistakes. Write the correct spelling for each word on the lines.

My sisters and I were playing a game of tip. Sofia was chaseing me down the sloppe when I tripped and scrapped my knee. Sally huried home to get the first aid back pack. She applyed some cream and put a plaster on the wound. The wound still smarted but I felt a lot batter. Once I felt reddy, we walked home.

______________ ______________ ______________ ______________

______________ ______________ ______________ ______________

Unit 8

Say Listen Look Understand Remember Practise	
itchy	______
witch	______
stitch	______
catch	______
hatch	______
watch	______
fetch	______
stretch	______
hutch	______
kitchen	______
My own words	
______	______
______	______

1 Write words with different first sounds.

w / d / st → itch ______ ______ ______

f / str → etch ______ ______

c / m / h → atch ______ ______ ______

2 Write words with different vowel sounds.

w – i / a – tch ______ ______

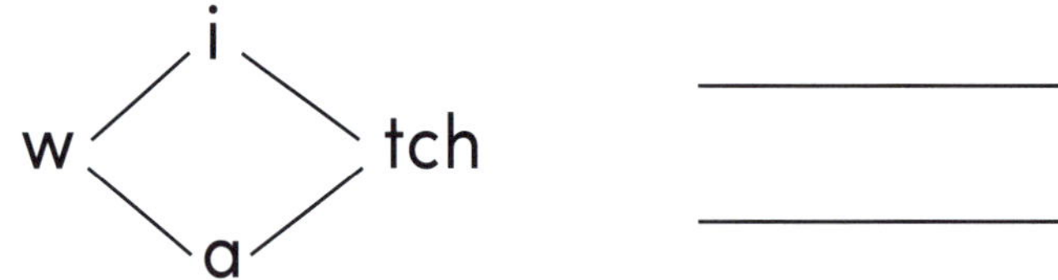

3 Write **ch** or **tch**.

swi______

______icken

______ur______

wi______

Tip

ch can begin or end a word.

tch can never begin a word.

Spelling Rules! Student Book 2 (ISBN 9780655092599) © Janelle Ho, Helen Pearson/Matilda Education Australia

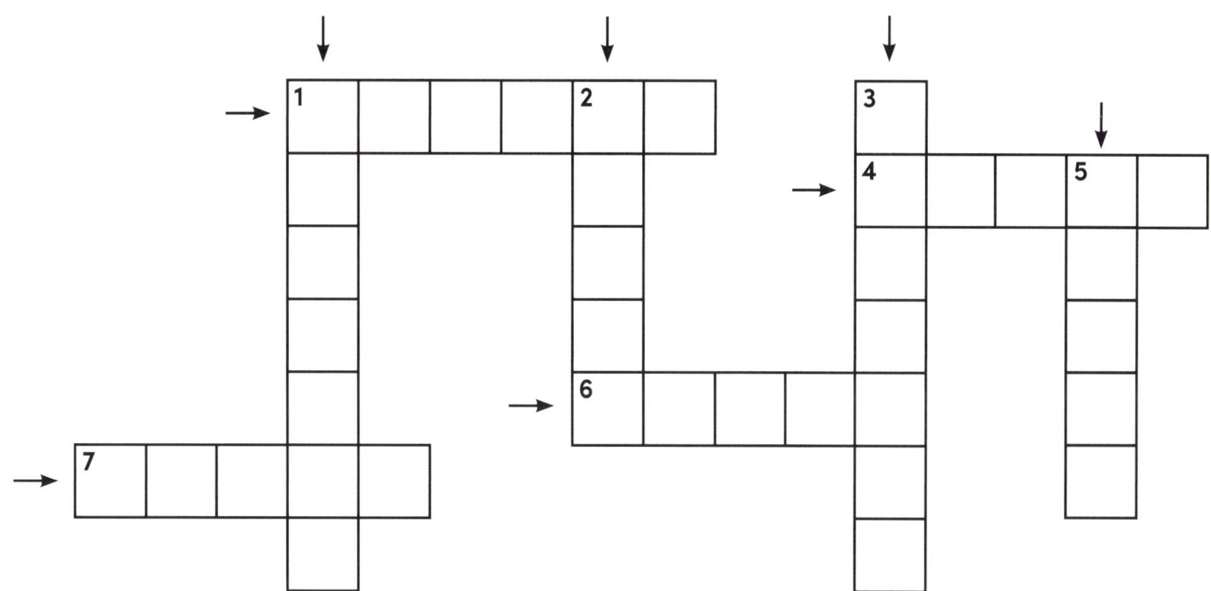

Use list words to complete the crossword puzzle.

Across →

1. A ____ in time saves nine.
4. The bite on my hand is ____.
6. A pet rabbit lives in a ____.
7. My dog likes to ____ sticks.

Down ↓

1. Always ____ before you exercise.
2. ____ the ball!
3. Dad is cooking in the ____.
5. When will the egg ____?

Write the right word.

witch = a woman who casts spells

which = asks for a particular one

A __________ turned my watch into a clock.

__________ switch turns on the porch light?

Words ending in **tch** add **es** to make the plural.

Write the plural.

match __________

watch __________

patch __________

Reflection

I can do this.

I am not sure.

I need help.

Unit 9

Say Listen Look Understand Remember Practise	
edge	______
hedge	______
badge	______
fridge	______
bridge	______
judge	______
smudge	______
dodge	______
fidget	______
gadget	______
My own words	
______	______
______	______

1  Write the words.

br, fr > idge ______ ______

f, j, sm > udge ______ ______ ______

h, l, w > edge ______ ______ ______

b < a, u > dge ______ ______

2  Use each clue to find a new word.

Rearrange *gifted* if you can't sit still. ______

Rearrange *tagged* to get a useful device. ______

Add **g** to *bride* to cross the river. ______

Change one letter in *wedge* to make a living fence. ______

Spelling Rules! Student Book 2 (ISBN 9780655092599) © Janelle Ho, Helen Pearson/Matilda Education Australia

Rule

For words with the letter pattern **ge**, if a syllable has a long vowel sound, it is usually followed by **ge**.

siege *stage*

If a syllable has a short vowel sound, it usually has a consonant in front of **ge**.

judge *bridge* *edge* *cringe* *bulge*

3 Write **ge** or **dge** to complete each word.

he_____ ba_____ fri_____ smu_____ hin_____

chan_____ mer_____ pa_____ do_____ indul_____

4 Proofread this text. The text has five words that are incorrect. Circle the mistakes. Then write the correct spelling of the words in the boxes.

The hamburger took so long to cook that I began to figget. Finally it was ready. Even though I ate carefully around the edge of the lardge burger, the tomato fell out and smardged my shirt. I quickly got a spunge and cleaned the spot. I couldn't finish the burger so I put the leftovers in the frige.

5 Write one sentence using both words.

badge gadget

____

____

____

Reflection

I can do this.

I am not sure.

I need help.

Unit 10

Say Listen Look Understand Remember Practise	
for	______
fork	______
torn	______
short	______
sport	______
more	______
fore	______
shore	______
chore	______
explore	______
My own words	
______	______
______	______

1 Say each word. Write the consonants to complete the word.

__ or __

__ or __

__ or __

__ __ or __

__ __ ore

__ __ ore

2 Write a list word that rhymes.

pork ______

sort ______

horn ______

core ______

3 Write the two list words that are homophones.

______

______

4 Choose the correct homophone.

for = belonging to; in the direction of; over a period of time

fore = located at the front *four* = 4

Mr Nguyen has been teaching ________ ________ years.

When Farah is on stage, her talent comes to the ________.

Could you please buy an apple ________ me?

5 Say both words. Colour the correct one.

I enjoy playing | sport | spore | at school.

Justin fell over and | torn | tore | his shorts.

Babies | explore | explode | to learn about the world.

Grandma never says no to | move | more | pie!

6 Make compound words. Draw a picture of each.

fore — arm / head / finger

________ ________ ________

7 Write a sentence for each word. Can you use both words in one sentence?

chore
before

____

____

Reflection

- I can do this.
- I am not sure.
- I need help.

Unit 11

What did the rug say to the floor?

"I've got you covered!"

Say Listen Look Understand Remember Practise	
saw	___
draw	___
claw	___
straw	___
crawl	___
lawn	___
prawn	___
poor	___
door	___
floor	___
My own words	
___	___
___	___

1 Write words with different first sounds.

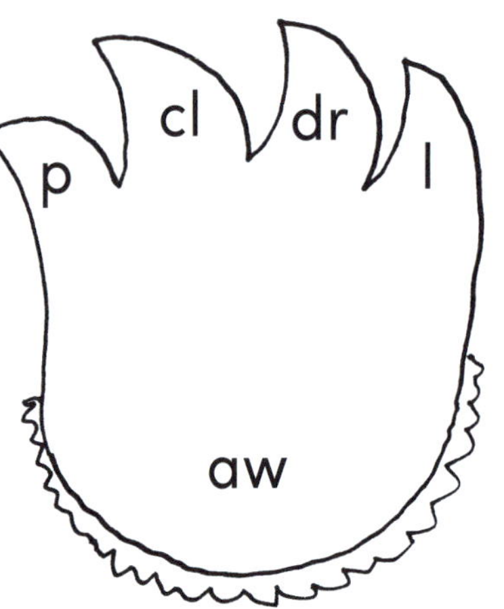

___

___

___

___

2 Circle the pictures with the same vowel sound as saw.

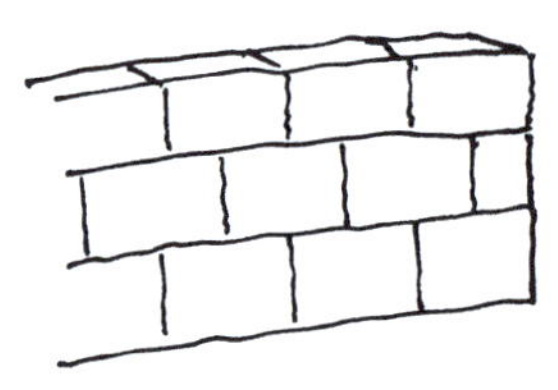

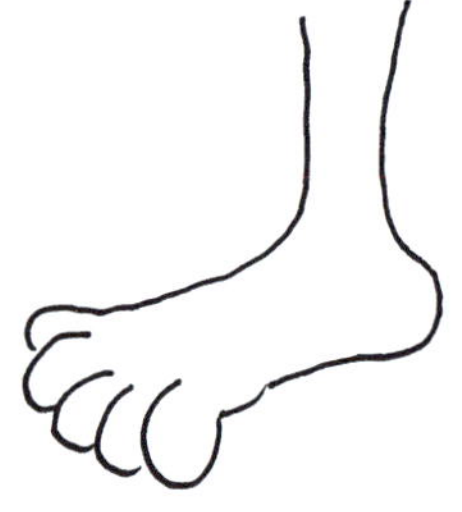

3 aw can be followed by a consonant. Write the words.

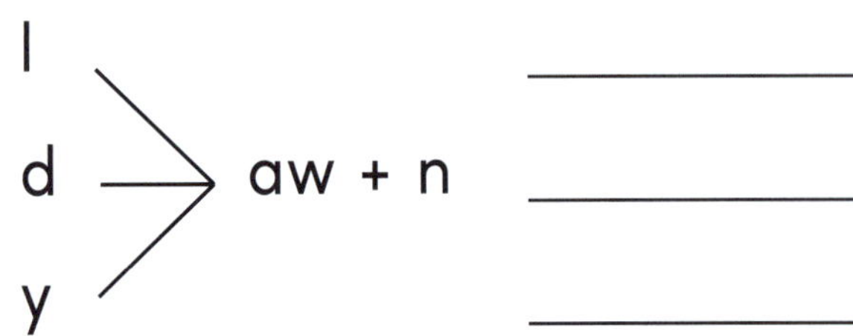

___

___

___

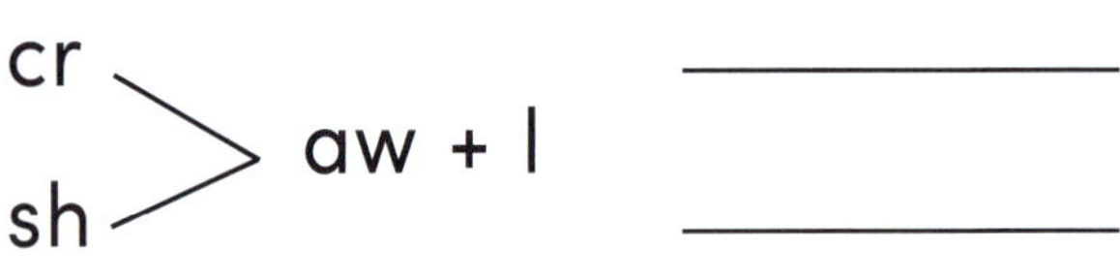

___

___

Spelling Rules! Student Book 2 (ISBN 9780655092599) © Janelle Ho, Helen Pearson/Matilda Education Australia

Say each word. Circle the word if it makes the same vowel sound as **aw**.

poor	blood	more	school	shore	choose
crow	four	door	for	floor	how

Draw a line to show the meaning for each homophone.

sore	hurting	paw	not rich
saw	looked at	poor	tip out of a jug
raw	loud sound	pour	an animal's foot
roar	not cooked	draw	sketch a picture
		drawer	place to put things

Colour the correct homophone.

The [paw | poor | pour] dog has hurt its [paw | poor | pour].

A dog with a [saw | sore] leg is sitting in a [draw | drawer].

Lions [raw | roar] when they smell [raw | roar] meat.

Write the list words in the correct group.

verb ________ ________ ________ ________

noun ________ ________ ________ ________

________ ________ ________

adjective ________

Which words are both a verb and a noun?

________ ________

Unit 12

Say Listen Look Understand Remember Practise	
war	____________
warn	____________
ward	____________
swarm	____________
award	____________
reward	____________
towards	____________
walk	____________
talk	____________
chalk	____________
My own words	
____________	____________
____________	____________

1 Circle the pictures that have the same vowel sound.

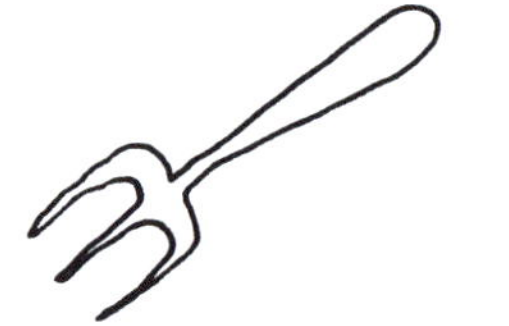

2 Write the word to match the picture.

w	
st	alk
ch	
t	

____________ 

____________ 

____________ 

____________ 

3 Use the words to make a wall.

war, warm, swarm

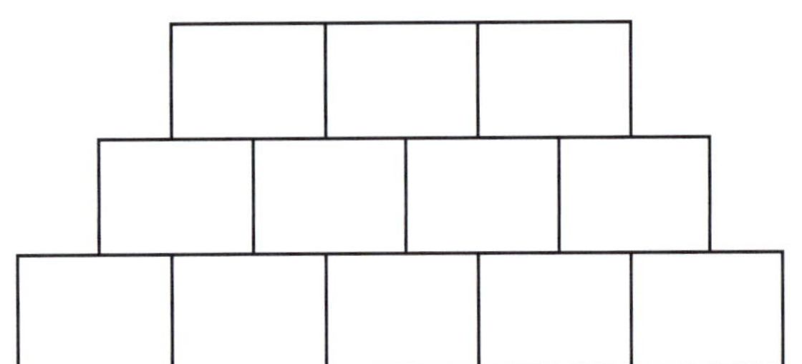

war, ward, award

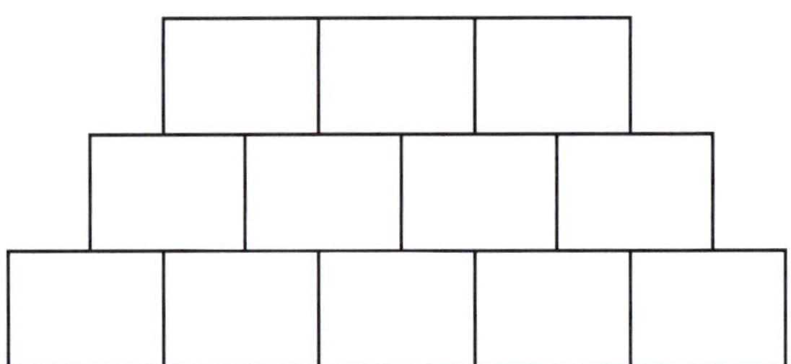

Spelling Rules! Student Book 2 (ISBN 9780655092599) © Janelle Ho, Helen Pearson/Matilda Education Australia

4 There are three list words that make new words when you write them backwards. Write the list word and the new word.

list word __________ __________ __________

new word __________ __________ __________

5 Add or change a letter to make a new word with a different vowel sound.

war ward warm

__________ __________ __________

6 Add or change a letter to make a new word with the same vowel sound.

walk talk

__________ __________

7 **-ward** and **-wards** are suffixes that indicate direction. Write the correct word in each sentence.

towards	forwards	backwards	upwards	downwards

A balloon filled with helium will go __________ quickly.

Push the coin firmly __________ to get a good mould.

The aim of chess is to defeat your opponent's king. To do this, you must move your chess pieces __________ your opponent's pieces. All the pieces can move __________. Only the pawn cannot move __________.

8 Use the words to describe what happens in your classroom. You may want to add **-s**, **-ed** or **-ing**.

talk ____________________

walk ____________________

chalk ____________________

Reflection

- I can do this.
- I am not sure.
- I need help.

Unit 13

Say Listen Look Understand Remember Practise	
ought	___
bought	___
brought	___
fought	___
thought	___
sought	___
caught	___
taught	___
naughty	___
daughter	___
My own words	
___	___
___	___

1  Write **au** or **ou**.

__ __ght	b __ __ght
br __ __ght	c __ __ght
d __ __ghter	f __ __ght
n __ __ghty	s __ __ght
t __ __ght	th __ __ght

Most verbs show the past tense by adding **ed**. Irregular verbs have a different form in the past tense.

see → saw

draw → drew

2  Write the list word that is the past tense.

buy	___	fight	___
teach	___	catch	___
bring	___	think	___

Spelling Rules! Student Book 2 (ISBN 9780655092599) © Janelle Ho, Helen Pearson/Matilda Education Australia

Antonyms are words with opposite meanings.

day, night *high, low* *lend, borrow*

Write the antonym.

sold	threw	cool	backwards	tall
________	________	________	________	________

Find the antonyms by circling the words that don't make sense.
Write the word with the opposite meaning.

It was midday on Christmas Eve. As there was no ____________
moon, it was very dark. Sam knew it was naughty but ____________
he fought to stay asleep. He once dreamed he had ____________
caught Santa Claus delivering presents. There was ____________
a soft crash outside and Sam jumped out of bed to ____________
shine his torch through the window. Two dull shiny eyes
blinked, then disappeared. It was just a possum. Sam
turned around to climb back into bed and gasped.
Leaning against his bed was a tiny package. It must be
the new bike he wanted. But how had it got there?

Write the noun for the family member.

Your mother is your grandmother's ____________.

Your mother's son is your ____________.

Your father's brother is your ____________.

Your father's sister is your ____________.

Reflection

 I can do this.

 I am not sure.

 I need help.

The same sound can be spelt in different ways. Write a word for each letter pattern that makes the sound **aw**.

aw as in straw and yawn

oor as in door and __________

or as in for and __________

ore as in core and __________

ar as in war and __________

al as in walk and __________

ough as in bought and __________

augh as in taught and __________

2 Use the clue to write the list word. What is the hidden word?

	Clue
1	not tall
2	present tense of *caught*
3	go on hands and knees
4	prize
5	speak
6	a job that is not pleasant
7	a home for a rabbit

What you do when you itch? ______________

3 Each word can be added to **walk** to make a compound word. Write the compound word to match the clue. You might need to add **-s** or **-ed**.

sleep	way	jay	about	space

Last night, Lulu ____________ to her brother's room.

Do not ____________. Use the zebra crossing.

William loves to go ____________ with his elders.

Have you seen videos of astronauts doing a ____________ ?

Please keep to the left along the ____________.

4 Add **-s** or **-es**.

badge ____________

reward ____________

stretch ____________

chore ____________

daughter ____________

gadget ____________

5 Add **-ing**.

snore ____________

catch ____________

judge ____________

explore ____________

fidget ____________

warn ____________

6 Take away one letter at a time to make a new word.

award	chore	prawn	sport
________	________	________	________
________	________	________	________
	________	________	

Unit 15

Say Listen Look Understand Remember Practise	
knife	______
knowledge	______
wrong	______
wrist	______
wriggle	______
listen	______
often	______
castle	______
bustle	______
whistle	______
My own words	
______	______
______	______

1 Say the word and look at the spelling. Circle the silent letter.

knee

listen

write

knot

castle

knight

2 Say the word. Colour the words with one syllable in purple. Colour the words with two syllables in orange.

bustle	castle	knife	knowledge	listen
often	whistle	wriggle	wrist	wrong

Spelling Rules! Student Book 2 (ISBN 9780655092599) © Janelle Ho, Helen Pearson/Matilda Education Australia

3 Write list words with the same silent letter. Then write a word of your own.

	write	kneel	castle
	______	______	______
	______	______	______
new word	______	______	______

4 Write all the words you can see in the worm.

two-letter words	three-letter words	four-letter words	five-letter words

5 Add a silent letter in each space.

The __ nob on the cas __ le door was the __ rong size.

I __ riggled through the bus __ ling crowd.

Mum scraped her __ nuckle with the __ nife.

She whis __ led and shook her __ rist to ease the pain.

Spelling Rules! Student Book 2 (ISBN 9780655092599)

Unit 16

Say Listen Look Understand Remember Practise	
pair	______
stair	______
chair	______
repair	______
airport	______
rare	______
share	______
square	______
bear	______
wear	______
My own words	
______	______
______	______

1 Write the list words in alphabetical order.

______
______
______
______
______
______
______
______
______
______

2 Proofread each sentence. Circle the mistake. Then write the correct spelling on the line.

Go up the stears to go to the teachers' room. ______

The squair slice is made of banana! ______

I need to ware my full school uniform tomorrow. ______

Spelling Rules! Student Book 2 (ISBN 9780655092599) © Janelle Ho, Helen Pearson/Matilda Education Australia

3 These words are irregular verbs. Use a dictionary to find the past tense.

tear ____________ wear ____________ bear ____________

4 Write the compound word to match the clue.

air + port air + line air + fare

the price you pay to fly on an aeroplane ____________

a company that provides flights ____________

an area for aeroplanes to land and take off ____________

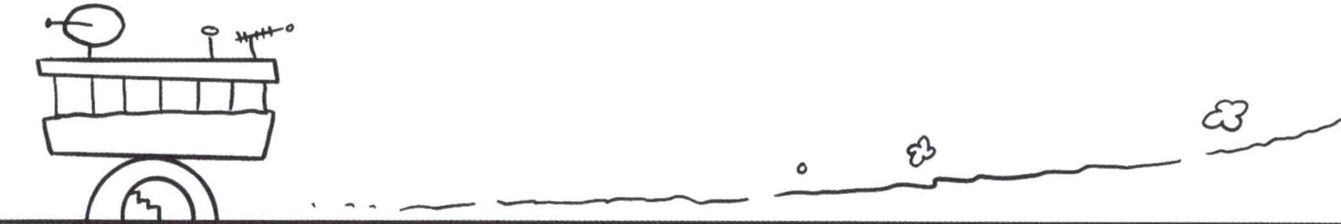

These words are homophones.

stare look at intensely *stair* a series of steps

bear withstand; also an animal *bare* without covering

wear put on clothes *where* a pronoun to show place

5 Colour the correct homophone.

I can't | bare | bear | seeing | bare | bear | trees in winter.

There are some places | where | wear | you can't | where | wear | shorts and thongs.

As the king came down the | stares | stairs |, everyone turned to | stare | stair |.

Spelling Rules! Student Book 2 (ISBN 9780655092599) © Janelle Ho, Helen Pearson/Matilda Education Australia

Unit 17

Say Listen Look Understand Remember Practise	
fear	________
hear	________
tear	________
clear	________
spear	________
weary	________
appear	________
deer	________
peer	________
cheer	________
queer	________
My own words	
________	________
________	________

1 Write the words.

f, h, n, y → ear
____
____
____
____

cl, sp → ear
____
____

d, j, p → eer
____
____
____

ch, qu, st → eer
____
____
____

2 Colour the circle brown if the word rhymes with **care**. Colour the circle blue if the word rhymes with **here**. Circle the word that can rhyme with both.

pear ◯ dear ◯ tear ◯

fear ◯ wear ◯ bear ◯

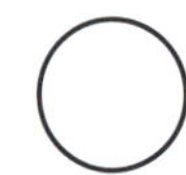

Spelling Rules! Student Book 2 (ISBN 9780655092599) © Janelle Ho, Helen Pearson/Matilda Education.

Words that have the same spelling but different meanings are **homographs**.

tear rip or force apart (rhymes with **care**)

tear a drop of water that falls from your eye (rhymes with **here**)

3 Use a dictionary to write the two meanings of these homographs.

wind 1 ____________________

2 ____________________

bow 1 ____________________

2 ____________________

4 Write the correct homophone on each line.

hear here	Come __________ so you can __________ the music more clearly.
deer dear	The paintings of the __________ are __________ to Dad. They were a present from Grandpa.

5 Write a story using the words in the box.

appear	queer

____

____

____

____

Reflection

- I can do this.
- I am not sure.
- I need help.

Unit 18

Say Listen Look Understand Remember Practise	
fern	___________
serve	___________
person	___________
perfect	___________
stir	___________
shirt	___________
first	___________
dirty	___________
thirsty	___________
birthday	___________
My own words	
___________	___________
___________	___________

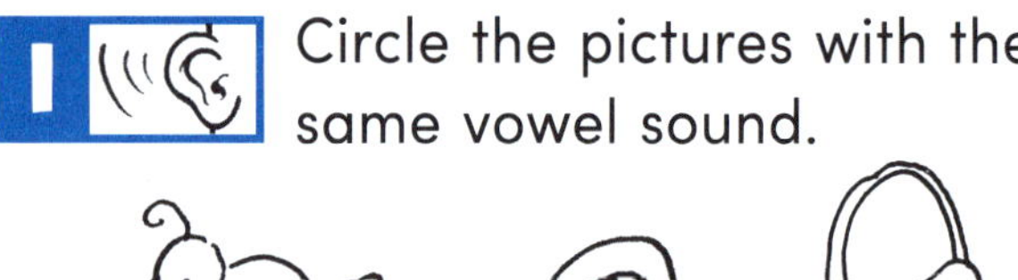

1 Circle the pictures with the same vowel sound.

2 Write **er** or **ir**. Use the list words to check.

s __ __ ve

st __ __

sh __ __ t

f __ __ st

d __ __ ty

b __ __ thday

3 Make as many words as you can.

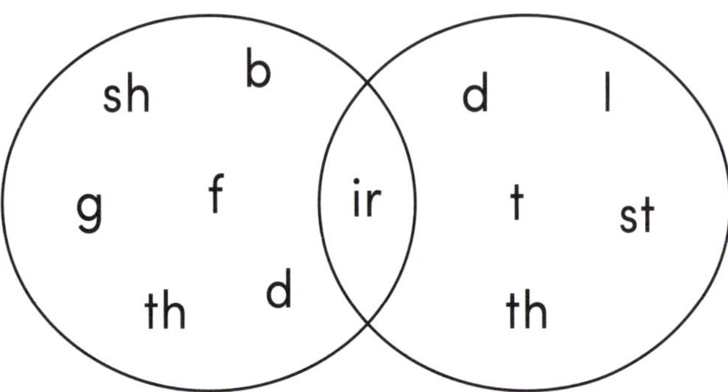

___________ ___________

___________ ___________

___________ ___________

___________ ___________

To compare two things, add **er** to the adjective.
dear → dearer

To compare three or more things, add **est**. *dear → dearest*

You may need to:

- double the last consonant to keep the vowel short
  hot → hottest
- drop the silent **e** *nice → nicest*
- change **y** to **i** *happy → happier, happiest*

4 Add **er** and **est**.

	dirty	safe	quiet	heavy
add **er**	______	______	______	______
add **est**	______	______	______	______

	big	dreamy	short	rare
add **er**	______	______	______	______
add **est**	______	______	______	______

5 Fix these crazy sentences. Write them again using a list word.

I need a drink of water because I am so hungry.

____

Josie scored 10 out of 10, a poor score.

____

Every adult animal is able to vote in an election.

____

Reflection

- I can do this.
- I am not sure.
- I need help.

Unit 19

How can you tell which end of a worm is its head?

Tickle it in the middle and see which end laughs.

Say Listen Look Understand Remember Practise	
turn	________
hurt	________
burst	________
nurse	________
curly	________
work	________
worth	________
learn	________
earth	________
search	________
My own words	
________	________
________	________

1 Write words with different first sounds.

b, t, ch → urn

____
____
____

p, n, c → urse

____
____
____

2 Write words with different last sounds.

wor → d, k, m, th, se

____
____
____
____
____

3 Say each word. Circle the words that have a different vowel sound.

word	cure	born	earth	fur
pear	burn	pearl	worm	learn

Spelling Rules! Student Book 2 (ISBN 9780655092599) © Janelle Ho, Helen Pearson/Matilda Education Australia

Use the clues to change Word 1 to Word 2.

Word 1	Clue	Word 2
ear	add two letters	We live on ____________.
curry	change one letter	Her hair is short and ____________.
fork	change one letter	Finish your ____________ quickly!
curl	change two letters	Ouch! I have ____________ my foot.
burn	change one letter and add one letter	Don't ____________ the balloons!
perch	change one letter and add one letter	I had to ____________ my room for my homework.

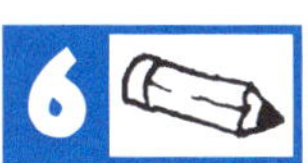

Write **ur**, **or** or **ear** words.

Mrs Worthington was surprised to find a ____________ in her ____________.

Gurjit wants to ____________ more about ____________ and other planets.

6 Answer the questions in full sentences.

What is your surname? ______________________________

What is your suburb? ______________________________

Use a dictionary to find two list words that do not change in the past tense.

____________ ____________

Reflection

- I can do this.
- I am not sure.
- I need help.

Unit 20

Say Listen Look Understand Remember Practise	
farmer	______
leader	______
dancer	______
shopper	______
follower	______
visitor	______
collector	______
editor	______
author	______
narrator	______
illustrator	______
My own words	
______	______
______	______

er and **or** at the end of a word often names an occupation or a job, or tells you what a person does.

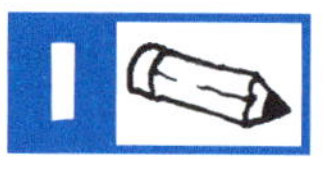

1 Write a list word to match the picture.

______ ______

______

______

2 Add **er** or **or**. Some are list words.

paint __ __	visit __ __	doct __ __	danc __ __
teach __ __	swimm __ __	collect __ __	edit __ __
shopp __ __	narrat __ __	carpent __ __	follow __ __

Spelling Rules! Student Book 2 (ISBN 9780655092599) © Janelle Ho, Helen Pearson/Matilda Education Australia

3 Sort the words into groups by the spelling rule.

baker jogger manager narrator robber winner

drop silent **e**	double last consonant

4 Write a list word.

The book's ______________ is Hugh Blewett.

The ______________ is Annette N'Post.

Its ______________ is a soccer player.

I Missed the Goal!
by
Hugh Blewett
Drawings
by
Annette
N'Post

5 Write a job or occupation, or what the person does.

I am the captain of the team. I am the ________________.

I make clothes. I am a ________________.

I work in a hospital. I examine people and tell them what is wrong and how they can get better. I am a ________________. I work with a ________________.

I find and keep stamps. I am a stamp ________________.

6 Write about what your mother or father does.

____

____

____

Reflection

I can do this.

I am not sure.

I need help.

Unit 21 Revision

1 Add consonants to change the vowel sound. Make two words each.

	+ 1 consonant		+ 2 consonants	
ear	______	______	______	______
are	______	______	______	______

2 Write the missing letters.

ch _ _ _

sq _ _ _ _

sh _ _ t

n _ _ se

b _ _ r

rep _ _ _

ch _ _ _

c _ _ ly

3 Write the name for these parts of your body.

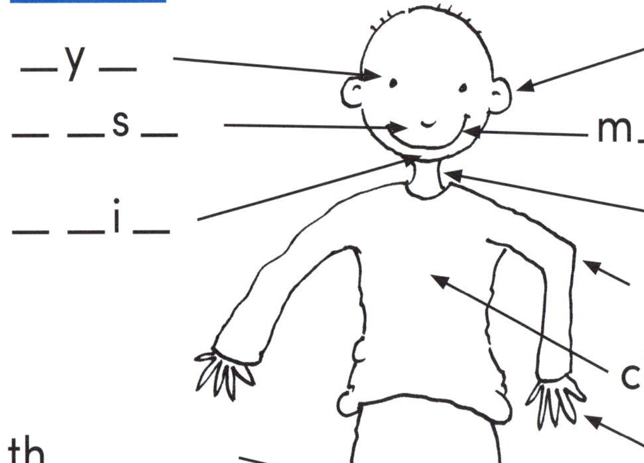

4 Add **ed**. Remember your spelling rules.

listen ______

share ______

stir ______

search ______

wriggle ______

appear ______

cheer ______

Circle the homograph in the sentence. Write a word that rhymes.

My baby brother doesn't know it is wrong to tear the pages in a book. ____________

Grandma has an old watch that she had to wind every day.

____

Anya tied a pretty bow around the doll's neck. ____________

Proofread this story. The story has five words that are incorrect. Circle the mistakes. Then write the correct spelling of the words in the clouds.

It is raining. Tony and his dad have to go to the areport to meet some visiters. They are Dad's friends. One of them is a writor who wants to learn about castels in Europe. Dad nose he will take a longer time to get there if it keeps raining. Hooray! The rain has stopped.

7 Write about your perfect day.

____

____

____

____

Unit 22

Say Listen Look Understand Remember Practise	
redo	________
reread	________
rejoin	________
reunite	________
unkind	________
unfair	________
untidy	________
disagree	________
disappear	________
disobey	________
My own words	
________	________
________	________

Rule **re**, **un** and **dis** are prefixes. A prefix comes before the base word. When you add a prefix, do not remove any letter.

1 Write the prefix and the base word.

redo = ________ + ________

reread = ________ + ________

rejoin = ________ + ________

reunite = ________ + ________

unkind = ________ + ________

unfair = ________ + ________

untidy = ________ + ________

disagree = ________ + ________

disappear = ________ + ________

disobey = ________ + ________

2 Look at the list words. Write the meaning of each prefix.

re ________________________________

un ________________________________

dis ________________________________

3 Add **re**, **un** or **dis**.

____ act	____ approve	____ lucky	____ abled
____ healthy	____ like	____ known	____ count

Tip

Synonyms are words with the same meaning.
Small, *little* and *tiny* are synonyms.

4 Write a list word that is a synonym.

messy ______________ differ or argue ______________

vanish ______________ mean or cruel ______________

5 Write a word with a prefix **re**, **un** or **dis**.

I love watching the sun ______________ over the horizon.

Jamal has to ______________ his schoolbag after school every day.

Rita's team lost. Of course, she felt ______________.

I like to ______________ my favourite part of the show so I can watch it again and again.

Mum swims because she doesn't like being ______________.

6 Write a sentence with a list word that uses the prefix **re**.
Can you use two?

____

____

____

Reflection

I can do this.

I am not sure.

I need help.

Unit 23

What happens when two snails have a fight?

Say Listen Look Understand Remember Practise	
lung	______
pluck	______
under	______
love	______
done	______
above	______
front	______
month	______
among	______
money	______
My own words	
______	______
______	______

l, r, fl, cl, str → ung

______
______
______
______
______

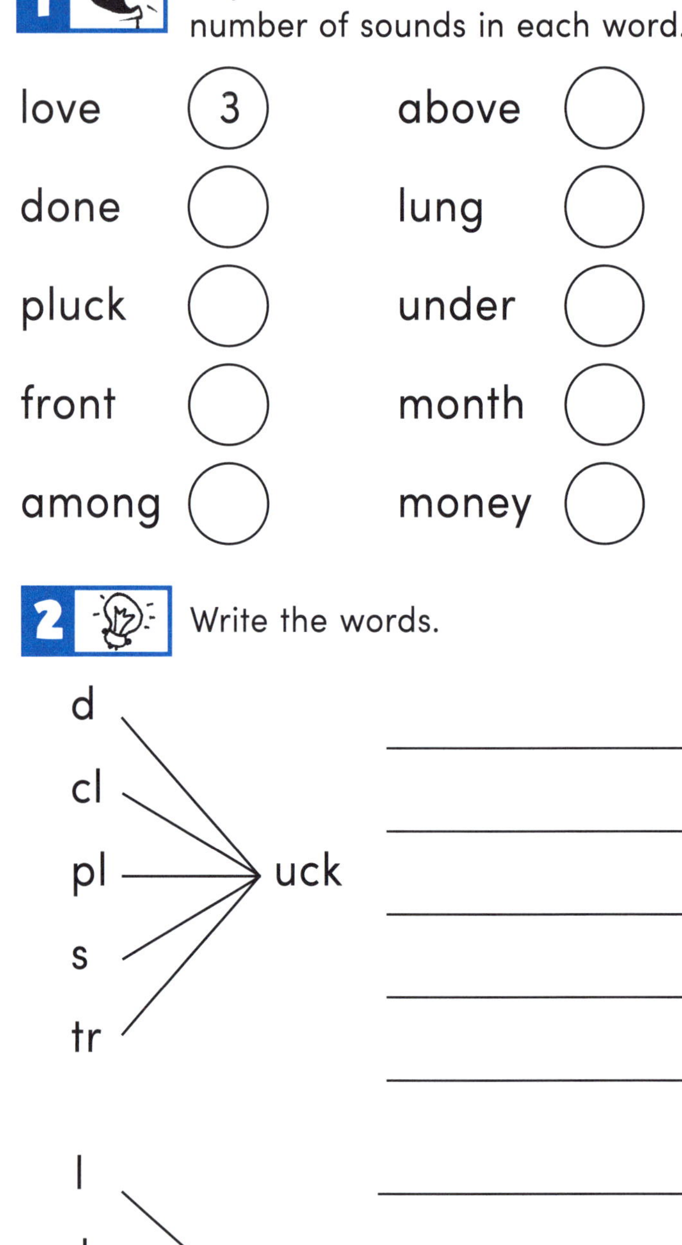

1 Say each word. Write the number of sounds in each word.

love	3	above	
done		lung	
pluck		under	
front		month	
among		money	

2 Write the words.

d, cl, pl, s, tr → uck

______
______
______
______
______

l, d, sh, c → ove

______
______
______
______

Circle the word that has a different sound.

Spelling Rules! Student Book 2 (ISBN 9780655092599) © Janelle Ho, Helen Pearson/Matilda Education Australia

3 Write a list word that fits in the group.

time	**place**	________
day	back	coin
________	side	dollar
year	________	cents

Tip

A **preposition** is a word that shows how things are related to each other. It comes before a noun. *under*, *above* and *among* are prepositions.

4 Use the picture to write the correct preposition.

There is a frog ________ the hat.

I love being ________ my friends.

The monkey hanging ________ the tree has a banana ________ its paw.

I sleep on the bottom bunk. My sister sleeps ________ me.

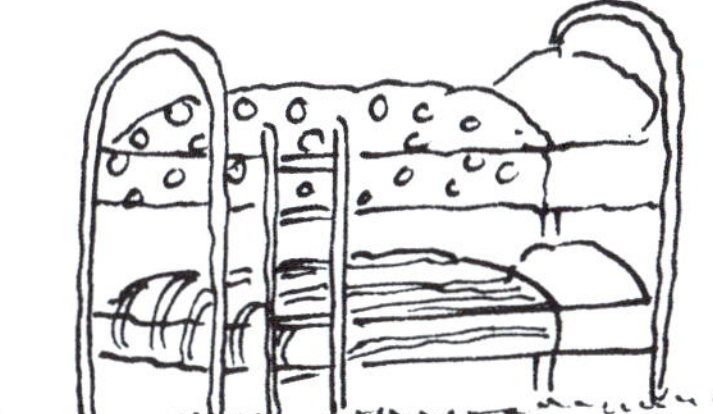

Karim placed the photo of the tree ________ the photo of the dog.

Reflection

- I can do this.
- I am not sure.
- I need help.

Unit 24

Say Listen Look Understand Remember Practise	
young	______
touch	______
cousin	______
country	______
double	______
rough	______
tough	______
enough	______
flood	______
blood	______
My own words	
______	______
______	______

1 Circle the words that have the same vowel as **duck**.

2 Write a list word that rhymes.

much ______

bubble ______

bud ______

puff ______

lung ______

3 Add **er** or **est** to complete the sentences.

Lucy wants to show she is ______ than her sister.
tough

Hari is the ______ of three children.
young

Which tree has the ______ bark?
rough

Spelling Rules! Student Book 2 (ISBN 9780655092599) © Janelle Ho, Helen Pearson/Matilda Education Australia

4 Answer these questions using complete sentences.

Which country do you live in?

____

Which Aboriginal country do you live in?

____

Tip

Antonyms are words with the opposite meaning.
Small and *big* are antonyms.

5 Write a word that is an antonym.

old	____________	smooth	____________	back	____________
over	____________	hate	____________	weak	____________

6 Proofread these sentences. Every sentence has one incorrect word. Circle the mistake. Then write the correct spelling.

You need to give bread dough enof time to rise. It should dubble in size. Then, when you tuche it, it should feel soft.

____________ ____________ ____________

My cussin is visiting from the country. He luves the life there, even if it is tough. ____________ ____________

Unit 25

Say Listen Look Understand Remember Practise	
joyful	
useful	
playful	
cheerful	
helpful	
careful	
painful	
awful	
colourful	
beautiful	
My own words	

1 Add **ful** to these words.

joy
play
help
harm
→ ful

use
care
hope
peace
→ ful

2 Words for quantities sometimes end in **ful**. *Handful* is an example. Use the pictures as clues to write these quantities.

3 Use the clue to find a list word to fit each sentence.

My nickname is Smiley as I am always ______________. (in a good mood)

Our classroom is bright and ______________. (has many colours)

Did you see the ______________ sunrise this morning? (pretty)

I baked the cake without sugar. It tasted ______________. (bad)

If a word ends in **y**, change **y** to **i** before adding **ful**.

duty → *dutiful*

Add **ful** to these words.

beauty → ______________ mercy → ______________

pity → ______________ plenty → ______________

A **mnemonic** is a trick to help us remember something.
Peace and *piece* are homophones.
The mnemonic *I'd like a piece of pie* can help you remember the difference.

Make your own mnemonic. You can use the underlined part as a hint.

careful ______________________________

colourful ______________________________

Spelling Rules! Student Book 2 (ISBN 9780655092599) © Janelle Ho, Helen Pearson/Matilda Education Australia

Unit 26

Say Listen Look Understand Remember Practise	
sadly	______
loudly	______
slowly	______
nicely	______
rudely	______
quickly	______
quietly	______
crossly	______
kindly	______
happily	______
My own words	
______	______
______	______

Adverbs tell us more about verbs.

Adverbs often end in **ly**.

1 Make adverbs by adding **ly**.

proud, soft, sad, quick, strong → ly

______
______
______
______
______

2 Add **ly** to these words.

nice → ______

rude → ______

safe → ______

If the word ends with a short **y**, change **y** to **i** before you add **ly**.

If the word ends with a long **y**, just add **ly**.

3 Follow the rules to add **ly**.

short y	change y to i + ly
happy	

long y	add ly
shy	

Spelling Rules! Student Book 2 (ISBN 9780655092599) © Janelle Ho, Helen Pearson/Matilda Education Australia

4 Use the sound in the base word to group the list words.

long vowel as in slowly

__________ __________ __________ __________

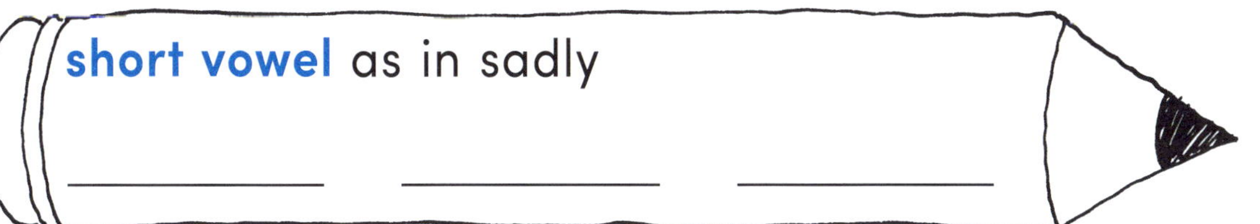

short vowel as in sadly

__________ __________ __________

Which word has a long and a short vowel? qu_ _ _ _ _

5 Write an adverb from the list to go with each verb.

smile	__________	whisper	__________
answer	__________	shout	__________
stroll	__________	grab	__________
run	__________	share	__________

6 Rewrite each sentence using an adverb instead of the underlined words. Don't forget the full stops.

The postman spoke to me <u>in a cross voice</u>.

____

____

I patted the dog <u>in a kind way</u>.

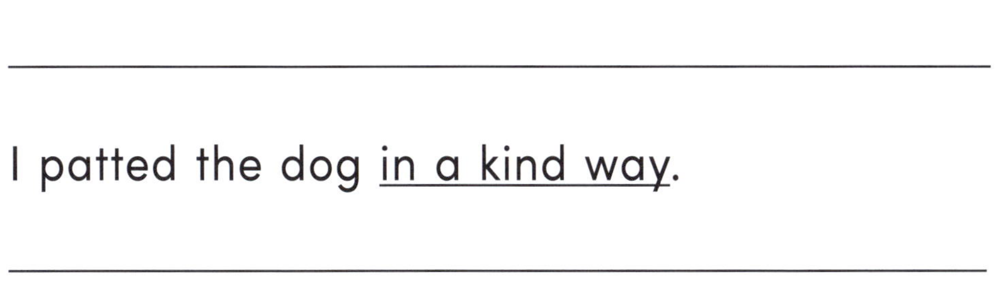

____

____

Reflection

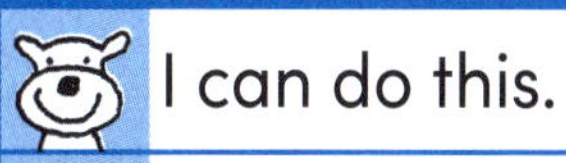

I can do this.

I am not sure.

I need help.

Unit 27

Say Listen Look Understand Remember Practise	
Sunday	________
Monday	________
Tuesday	________
Wednesday	________
Thursday	________
Friday	________
Saturday	________
today	________
tomorrow	________
because	________
My own words	
________	________
________	________

1 The days of the week are often abbreviated. Write the full name for each day.

Fri. ________

Tues. ________

Mon. ________

Sat. ________

Wed. ________

2 Which days start with the same letter?

S ________ T ________

S ________ T ________

3 What day is it?

Today is ________.

Yesterday was ________.

Tomorrow is ________.

4 Look up a calendar for this year and write the day of the week for each celebration.

This year New Year's Day was on ________.

This year Anzac Day was on ________.

This year my birthday ________.

NAIDOC Week begins on ________.

Spelling Rules! Student Book 2 (ISBN 9780655092599) © Janelle Ho, Helen Pearson/Matilda Education Australia

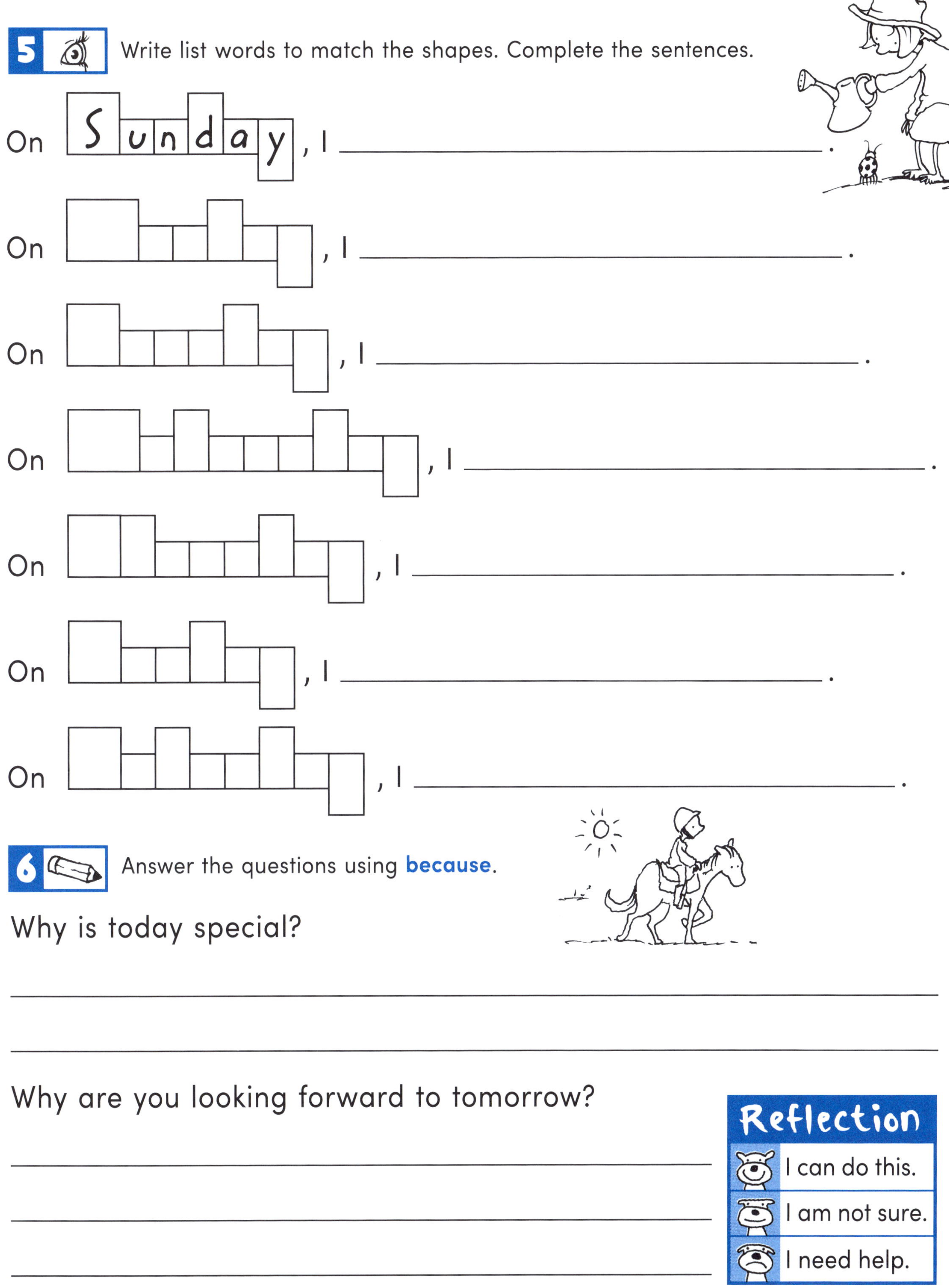

5 Write list words to match the shapes. Complete the sentences.

On Sunday, I ______________________________.

On __________, I ______________________________.

On __________, I ______________________________.

On __________, I ______________________________.

On __________, I ______________________________.

On __________, I ______________________________.

On __________, I ______________________________.

6 Answer the questions using **because**.

Why is today special?

____

____

Why are you looking forward to tomorrow?

____

____

____

Reflection

I can do this.

I am not sure.

I need help.

What is easy to get into but difficult to get out of?

1 Write a list word that rhymes. Change the vowel.

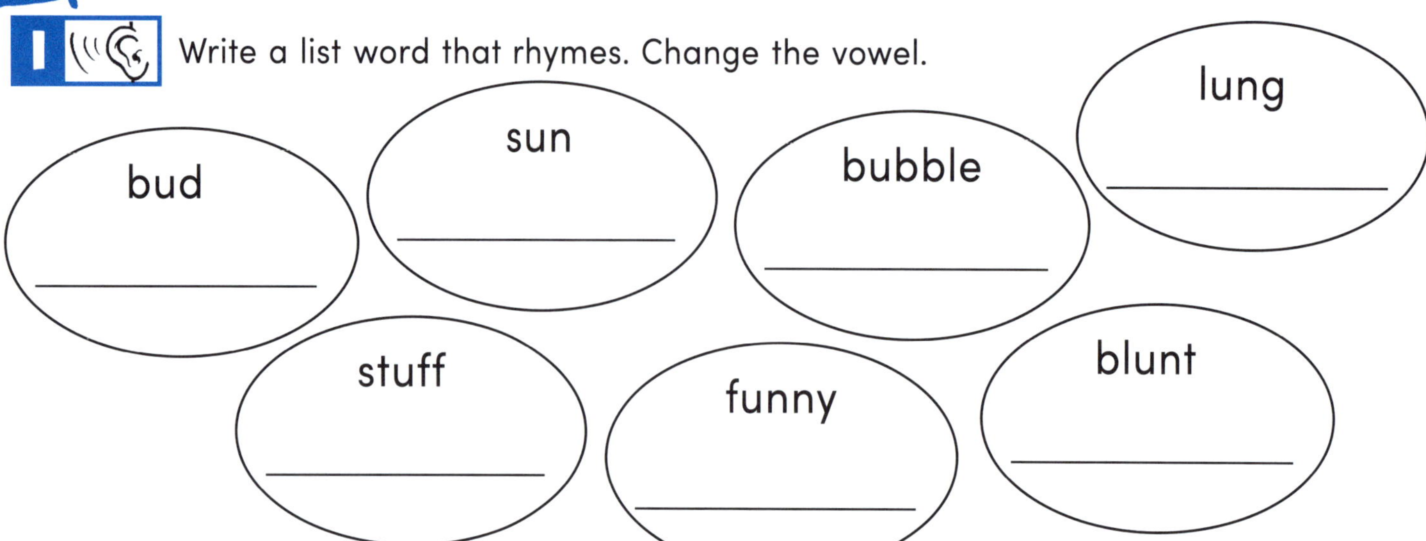

2 Add **un** or **dis** to make the opposite word.

_____happy _____agree _____likely _____tidy

_____obey _____do _____clear _____approve

3 Use the clues to change Word 1 to Word 2.

Word 1	Clue	Word 2
money	add one letter	You're a cheeky _____________!
mouth	change one letter	My favourite _____________ is December.
count	add two letters	Sydney is located in Gadigal _____________.
touch	change one letter	The meat is as _____________ as a boot.

4 Write a word beginning with the prefix **re**. You may need to add a suffix.

I _____________ my favourite book once a term.

We were thrilled that Danny _____________ our team this term.

Spelling Rules! Student Book 2 (ISBN 9780655092599) © Janelle Ho, Helen Pearson/Matilda Education Australia

Add **ly** to each word.

quick → ________ clever → ________

nice → ________ strong → ________

happy → ________ thirsty → ________

Add **ful** and **ly** to each word.

play + ful + ly = ________

cheer + ful + ly = ________

care + ful + ____ = ________

faith + ful + ____ = ________

peace + ____ + ____ = ________

beauty + ____ + ____ = ________

Add a day of the week and **because** to complete each sentence.

I dislike ________ ________.
day

I like ________ ________.
day

Change only one letter at a time to make the new word.

hand	son	stare
________	________	________
________	________	________
care	buy	short

Unit 29

Say Listen Look Understand Remember Practise	
foggy	______
along	______
belong	______
toffee	______
homophone	______
wasp	______
wand	______
watch	______
wander	______
sausage	______
My own words	
______	______
______	______

1 Write the missing letters.

t __ ffee

w __ nd

bel __ ng

f __ ggy

w __ tch

s __ __ sage

2 Say the word. Circle the pictures that have a short **o** sound.

3 Write the words. Highlight the word if the vowel sound is different from the list word.

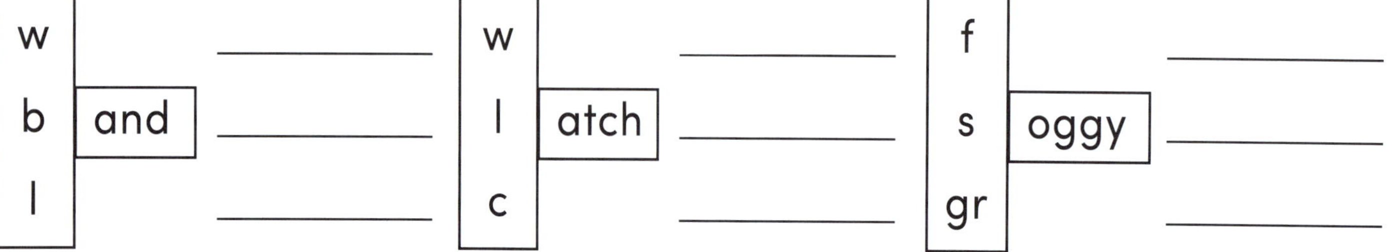

Spelling Rules! Student Book 2 (ISBN 9780655092599) © Janelle Ho, Helen Pearson/Matilda Education Australia

4 Write the plural.

wand ____________ homophone ____________

wasp ____________ sausage ____________

watch ____________ toffee ____________

5 Draw a line between each syllable. The first one has been done for you.

a / long belong toffee wander homophone

6 Find small words in each list word.

belong	wasp	toffee	homophone
________	________	________	________
________	________	________	________
		________	________
		________	________

7 Answer the questions.

Sea and **see** are homophones. What does **homophone** mean?

____

Tear is a homograph. What does **homograph** mean (see page 39)?

____

Unit 30

What do you get when you cross a lion with a rose?

I **don't** know, but I **wouldn't** try smelling it!

Say Listen Look Understand Remember Practise	
I'll	________
he's	________
it's	________
isn't	________
can't	________
don't	________
doesn't	________
didn't	________
won't	________
we're	________
My own words	
________	________
________	________

Rule

A **contraction** is the short form of a word or words. Use an **apostrophe** to show that letters have been left out.

I will ⟶ I'll
it is ⟶ it's
do not ⟶ don't

1  Circle the words that match each short form.

I'm	I can I am I must
he's	he is he was he does
isn't	is not it is does not
can't	care not can I cannot
won't	what is will not what not

2 The window shows which letters must be taken away. Write the short word that comes out of the shrinking machine.

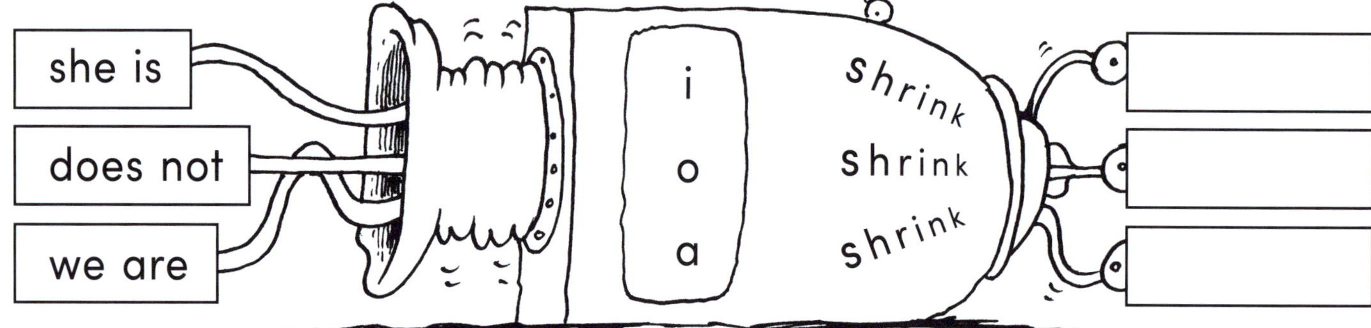

3 Write list words to complete the story.

"May I please go to Alex's house, Mum?" I asked. "No, you ________," Mum said. "________ Grandad's birthday today and we ________ want to go to his party without a present. So ________ going to the shops now and I need you to help me choose his gift."

4 **His** and **he's** are often confused. Colour the correct word in each sentence.

Ali packed | his | he's | bag before going to bed.

Don't annoy Annan while | his | he's | working.

5 **They're**, **their** and **there** are often confused. Colour the correct word in each sentence.

They're	Their	There	are hooks where they can hang wet raincoats.
They're	Their	There	raincoats were dry by the end of the day.
They're	Their	There	not allowed to use umbrellas.

6 Write your own sentence using **it's**. Make sure it means **it is**.

____

____

____

Reflection

- I can do this.
- I am not sure.
- I need help.

Unit 31

Say Listen Look Understand Remember Practise	
city	______
cent	______
scent	______
scene	______
once	______
cancel	______
cycle	______
cylinder	______
science	______
scissors	______
My own words	
______	______
______	______

Tip c is soft like s when the next letter is e, i or y.

1 Listen to the sound c makes in each list word. Write the word inside the correct shape.

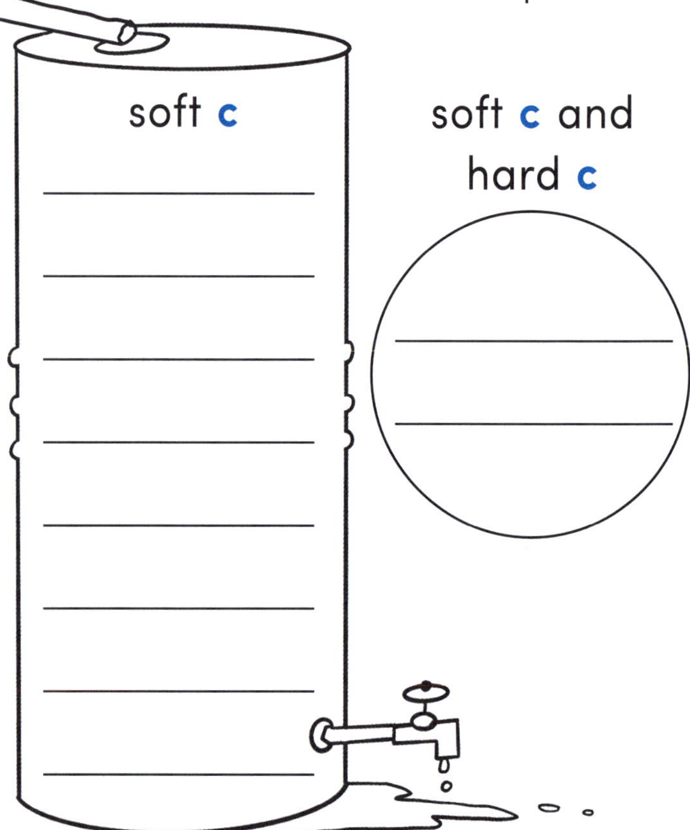

2 Say the word. Circle the fruit or vegetable that has a soft c sound.

capsicum

cucumber

lettuce

carrot

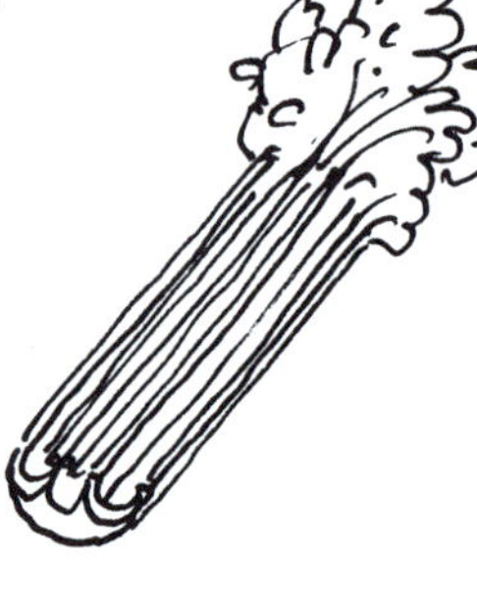

celery

3 The missing letters all make an **s** sound. Write **c** or **s**.

___illy ___ity s___ent ___uper s___ien___e

dan___e bu___ ___ycle ___lime ___ircu___

4 Choose the correct homophone.

The | cent | scent | from the candle reminds me of the | sea | see |.

Guess what? I | one | won | | one | won | hundred | cents | scents |!

Were you at the | seen | scene | when the kangaroos hopped into town? I have never | seen | scene | anything like it!

5 Write your own beginning for a fairy tale.

Once upon a time ________________________________

____

____

____

____

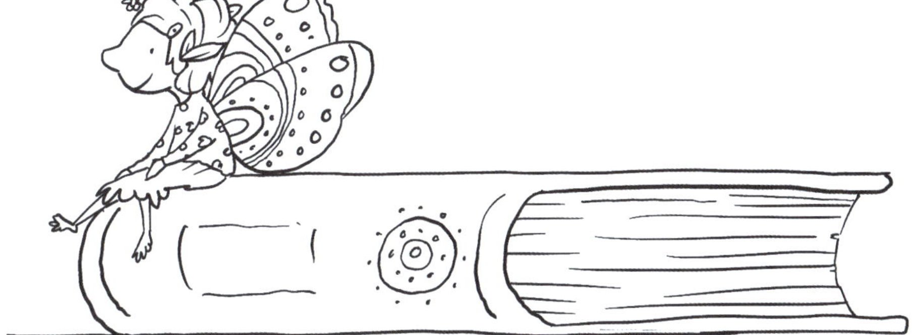

Unit 32

Say Listen Look Understand Remember Practise	
lamb	______
limb	______
dumb	______
numb	______
thumb	______
comb	______
climb	______
autumn	______
column	______
plumber	______
My own words	
______	______
______	______

1 Silent letters are usually part of a letter pattern. Make words with a silent letter.

la / du / co / cli → mb
______
______
______
______

autu / colu → mn
______
______

kn → ow / ife / ock
______
______
______

wr → ong / eck / ite
______
______
______

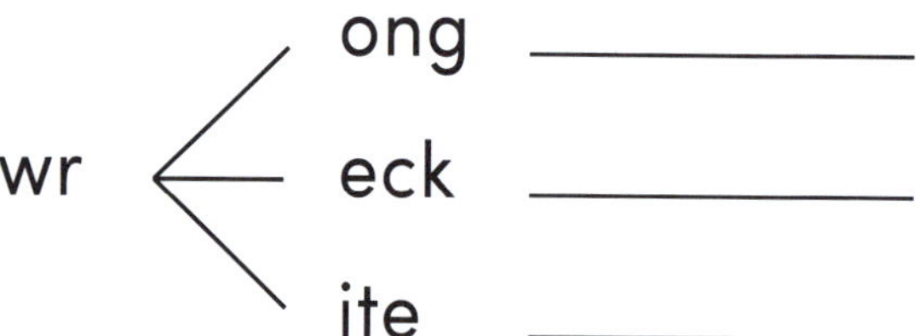

2 Write the letters to make a list word. Circle the silent letter.

la__ __

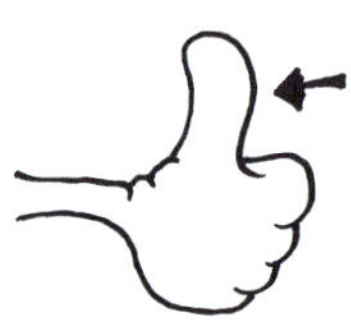

thu__ __

colu__ __

cli__ __

Spelling Rules! Student Book 2 (ISBN 9780655092599) © Janelle Ho, Helen Pearson/Matilda Education Australia

Add the correct suffix to complete the sentence.

Dad had to call two plumber_____ to get our leak fixed.

Jen climb_____ the tree easily because its limb_____ were so low.

A year has four seasons: spring, summer, autumn and winter. Name the season in each picture. Then write one word to describe that season.

____

____

____

____

____

____

____

____

5 Use the clue to write a new word.

comb (c → t) _______________	limb (i → a) _______________
come (e → b) _______________	limp (p → b) _______________

Reflection

- I can do this.
- I am not sure.
- I need help.

Unit 33

What do you cast away when you need it and take back in when you don't?

Say Listen Look Understand Remember Practise	
school	______
ache	______
choir	______
character	______
chorus	______
chameleon	______
stomach	______
anchor	______
chef	______
machine	______
My own words	
______	______
______	______

1 Sort the list words into the correct group.

ch sounds like **k**

______ ______

______ ______

______ ______

______ ______

ch sounds like **sh**

______

______

2 Write the plural.

one choir, two ______

one character, two ______

one chorus, two ______

one machine, two ______

one ache, two ______

one chef, two ______

Spelling Rules! Student Book 2 (ISBN 9780655092599) © Janelle Ho, Helen Pearson/Matilda Education Australia

 Use the clue to write a list word.

a person in a story ________________

an animal ________________

two words about singing ________________ ________________

a place that has "cool" inside ________________

something that rumbles when you're hungry ________________

a good person to have when you're hungry ________________

  Make compound words.

 + ache = ________________

 + ache = ________________

 + ache = ________________

 + ache = ________________

 What are you looking forward to in the school holidays?

____

____

____

____

____

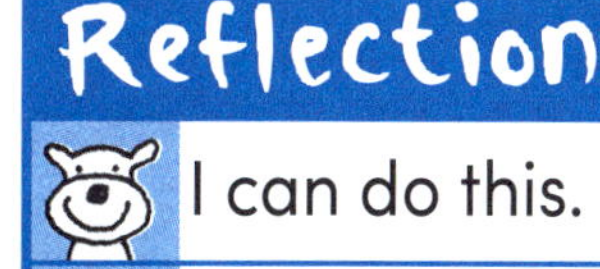

I need help.

Unit 34

What do you get if you cross a ghost with an elephant?

Say Listen Look Understand Remember Practise	
no one	______
nothing	______
nowhere	______
somebody	______
something	______
anyone	______
anything	______
another	______
everyone	______
everywhere	______
My own words	
______	______
______	______

1 Circle the word with a different first vowel sound.

nobody nothing nowhere

2 Draw a line to show the two words in each compound word.

somebody	everyone
nobody	anywhere
everywhere	nothing
anything	nowhere
somewhere	everything
anyone	sometimes
everybody	somehow

3 Make as many compound words as you can by adding another part.

some ______

______

where ______

______

BEWARE!

no one = two words

*I heard the doorbell ring but there is **no one** there!*

Write list words.

Old Mother Hubbard's cupboard is bare.

There is ____________ at all in there!

There is ____________ at the door. I think it's the plumber.

Mum! I can't find my football.

I've looked in the backyard.

I've looked in all the bedrooms.

I've looked ____________.

This glass is cracked. May I have ____________ one?

Use a dictionary to help you write these words in alphabetical order.

anywhere anyone anything anybody anyhow anyway

1. ____________ 2. ____________

3. ____________ 4. ____________

5. ____________ 6. ____________

I need help.

Write the missing letters.

_ _ nd

th _ _ _

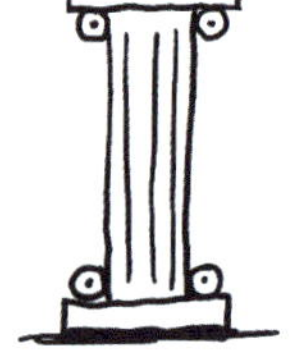

c _ lu _ _

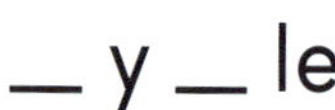

_ y _ le

_ _ ef

an _ _ _ _

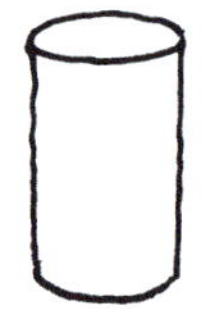

_ _ lind _ _

_ _ i _ _ ors

Follow the pattern.

carry	is	to	carries	as	hurry	is	to	______
splash	is	to	splashes	as	watch	is	to	______
shine	is	to	shining	as	write	is	to	______
blow	is	to	blew	as	throw	is	to	______
step	is	to	stepped	as	cancel	is	to	______
scrape	is	to	scraped	as	ache	is	to	______
boil	is	to	boiling	as	sail	is	to	______
funny	is	to	funniest	as	tidy	is	to	______

Write a word that is a homophone. Circle the one that has a silent letter.

paw	seen	stare	for	cent	night
______	______	______	______	______	______

Spelling Rules! Student Book 2 (ISBN 9780655092599) © Janelle Ho, Helen Pearson/Matilda Education Australia

4 Write the contraction.

I will ____________ cannot ____________

it is ____________ will not ____________

is not ____________ you are ____________

 Add a prefix and a suffix.

re + do + ing = ____________________

______ + kind + ______ = ____________________

______ + appear + ______ = ____________________

______ + agree + ______ = ____________________

  Write as many compound words as you can.

some ____

any ____

every ____

7 This is part of Jing's holiday timetable. What is happening each day?

Mon.	 	On ____________, Jing is ______________________.
Tues.		On ____________, Jing is ______________________.
Wed.		On ____________, Jing is ______________________.
Thurs.		On ____________, Jing is ______________________.
Fri.		On ____________, Jing is ______________________.

Unit 1
place
scrape
time
unite
slope
whole
complete
squeeze
rule
cure

Unit 2
beg
scan
clap
strap
swim
begin
block
throb
thud
scrub

Unit 3
lady
pony
busy
ready
sorry
worry
carry
hurry
reply
apply

Unit 4
arm
car
park
dark
star
start
hard
barn
smart
farmer

Unit 5
letter
little
bottle
rabbit
cuddle
riddle
ripple
tunnel
borrow
pillow

Unit 6
chicken
bucket
ticket
packet
pocket
jacket
cricket
bracket
backpack
limerick

Unit 8
itchy
witch
stitch
catch
hatch
watch
fetch
stretch
hutch
kitchen

Unit 9
edge
hedge
badge
fridge
bridge
judge
smudge
dodge
fidget
gadget

Unit 10
for
fork
torn
short
sport
more
fore
shore
chore
explore

Unit 11
saw
draw
claw
straw
crawl
lawn
prawn
poor
door
floor

Unit 12
war
warn
ward
swarm
award
reward
towards
walk
talk
chalk

Unit 13
ought
bought
brought
fought
thought
sought
caught
taught
naughty
daughter

Unit 15
knife
knowledge
wrong
wrist
wriggle
listen
often
castle
bustle
whistle

Unit 16
pair
stair
chair
repair
airport
rare
share
square
bear
wear

Unit 17
fear
hear
tear
clear
spear
weary
appear
deer
peer
cheer
queer

Unit 18
fern
serve
person
perfect
stir
shirt
first
dirty
thirsty
birthday

Unit 19
turn
hurt
burst
nurse
curly
work
worth
learn
earth
search

Unit 20
farmer
leader
dancer
shopper
follower
visitor
collector
editor
author
narrator
illustrator

Unit 22
redo
reread
rejoin
reunite
unkind
unfair
untidy
disagree
disappear
disobey

Unit 23
lung
pluck
under
love
done
above
front
month
among
money

Unit 24
young
touch
cousin
country
double
rough
tough
enough
flood
blood

Unit 25
joyful
useful
playful
cheerful
helpful
careful
painful
awful
colourful
beautiful

Unit 26
sadly
loudly
slowly
nicely
rudely
quickly
quietly
crossly
kindly
happily

Unit 27
Sunday
Monday
Tuesday
Wednesday
Thursday
Friday
Saturday
today
tomorrow
because

Unit 29
foggy
along
belong
toffee
homophone
wasp
wand
watch
wander
sausage

Unit 30
I'll
he's
it's
isn't
can't
don't
doesn't
didn't
won't
we're

Unit 31
city
cent
scent
scene
once
cancel
cycle
cylinder
science
scissors

Unit 32
lamb
limb
dumb
numb
thumb
comb
climb
autumn
column
plumber

Unit 33
school
ache
choir
character
chorus
chameleon
stomach
anchor
chef
machine

Unit 34
no one
nothing
nowhere
somebody
something
anyone
anything
another
everyone
everywhere

LIST WORDS IN ALPHABETICAL ORDER

above	Unit 23
ache	Unit 33
airport	Unit 16
along	Unit 29
among	Unit 23
anchor	Unit 33
another	Unit 34
anyone	Unit 34
anything	Unit 34
appear	Unit 17
apply	Unit 3
arm	Unit 4
author	Unit 20
autumn	Unit 32
award	Unit 12
awful	Unit 25
backpack	Unit 6
badge	Unit 9
barn	Unit 4
bear	Unit 16
beautiful	Unit 25
because	Unit 27
beg	Unit 2
begin	Unit 2
belong	Unit 29
birthday	Unit 18
block	Unit 2
blood	Unit 24
borrow	Unit 5
bottle	Unit 5
bought	Unit 13
bracket	Unit 6
bridge	Unit 9
brought	Unit 13
bucket	Unit 6
burst	Unit 19
bustle	Unit 15
busy	Unit 3
cancel	Unit 31
can't	Unit 30
car	Unit 4
careful	Unit 25
carry	Unit 3
castle	Unit 15
catch	Unit 8
caught	Unit 13
cent	Unit 31
chair	Unit 16
chalk	Unit 12
chameleon	Unit 33
character	Unit 33
cheer	Unit 17
cheerful	Unit 25
chef	Unit 33
chicken	Unit 6
choir	Unit 33
chore	Unit 10
chorus	Unit 33
city	Unit 31
clap	Unit 2
claw	Unit 11
clear	Unit 17
climb	Unit 32
collector	Unit 20
colourful	Unit 25
column	Unit 32
comb	Unit 32
complete	Unit 1
country	Unit 24
cousin	Unit 24
crawl	Unit 11
cricket	Unit 6
crossly	Unit 26
cuddle	Unit 5
cure	Unit 1
curly	Unit 19
cycle	Unit 31
cylinder	Unit 31
dancer	Unit 20
dark	Unit 4
daughter	Unit 13
deer	Unit 17
didn't	Unit 30
dirty	Unit 18
disagree	Unit 22
disappear	Unit 22
disobey	Unit 22
dodge	Unit 9
doesn't	Unit 30
done	Unit 23
don't	Unit 30
door	Unit 11
double	Unit 24
draw	Unit 11
dumb	Unit 32
earth	Unit 19
edge	Unit 9
editor	Unit 20
enough	Unit 24
everyone	Unit 34
everywhere	Unit 34
explore	Unit 10
farmer	Unit 4
fear	Unit 17
fern	Unit 18
fetch	Unit 8
fidget	Unit 9
first	Unit 18
flood	Unit 24
floor	Unit 11
foggy	Unit 29
follower	Unit 20
for	Unit 10
fore	Unit 10
fork	Unit 10
fought	Unit 13
Friday	Unit 27
fridge	Unit 9
front	Unit 23
gadget	Unit 9
happily	Unit 26
hard	Unit 4
hatch	Unit 8
hear	Unit 17
hedge	Unit 9
helpful	Unit 25
he's	Unit 30
homophone	Unit 29
hurry	Unit 3
hurt	Unit 19
hutch	Unit 8
I'll	Unit 30
illustrator	Unit 20
isn't	Unit 30
itchy	Unit 8
it's	Unit 30
jacket	Unit 6
joyful	Unit 25
judge	Unit 9
kindly	Unit 26
kitchen	Unit 8
knife	Unit 15
knowledge	Unit 15
lady	Unit 3
lamb	Unit 32
lawn	Unit 11
leader	Unit 20
learn	Unit 19
letter	Unit 5
limb	Unit 32
limerick	Unit 6
listen	Unit 15
little	Unit 5
loudly	Unit 26
love	Unit 23
lung	Unit 23

Spelling Rules! Student Book 2 (ISBN 9780655092599) © Janelle Ho, Helen Pearson/Matilda Education Australia

SPELLING RULES AND TIPS

A **prefix** is added to the beginning of a word; **re**, **un** and **dis** are prefixes

A **suffix** is added to the end of a word; **s**, **es**, **ed**, **ing**, **er**, **est**, **ful** and **ly** are suffixes.

To make a plural

When a word ends in **s**, **x**, **ss**, **sh** or **ch**, add **es**.

buses foxes dresses brushes lunches

When a word ends in a consonant followed by **y**, change **y** to **i**, then add **es**.

baby → babies

When a word ends in a vowel followed by **y**, add **s** only.

day → days

When a word ends in silent **e**, drop the **e** before adding **ed**, **ing**, **er** or **est**.

smile → smiled care → caring bake → baker

If a word has a short vowel sound, double the final consonant before adding **ed**, **ing**, **er** or **est**.

pat → patted slip → slipping big → bigger

If a word ends with a short **y**, change **y** to **i** before adding **ed**, **er**, **est**, **ful** or **ly**.

tidy → tidied beauty → beautiful happy → happily

A word that has been shortened by leaving out some of the letters is called a **contraction**. An apostrophe is used to show that letters have been left out.

I will → I'll it is → it's do not → don't